Candyman
Simone Poirier-Bures

Dec/94

For Sandra —
I hope you enjoy this
"trip" to Nova Scotia.
all the best,
Simone Poirier-Bures

This book was published with the assistance of the Canada Council, the Ontario Arts Council and others.

"One Last Time" appeared in a slightly different version in *The Dalhousie Review*. "This Thing Between Men and Women" was published in a different form in *Belles Lettres*. Parts of "Saturday Night" first appeared in *Moving Out*. "Blue Coat" was first published in *Catholic Girls and Boys*.

ISBN 0 88750 977 0 (hardcover)
ISBN 0 88750 978 9 (softcover)

Cover art by Mendelson Joe, photograph by David Smiley
Book design by Michael Macklem

Printed in Canada

PUBLISHED IN CANADA BY OBERON PRESS

For Arthur L.
And for my mother, Léonie Comeau Poirier, without whose encouragement and example I might never have become a writer.

1: New Beginnings

Someone is coming down the street. Nicole squints at the tall figure, at the brown fedora and suit, at the big leather briefcase. It's him! Annette grabs her hand and they rush up the gravel road. They have been waiting and waiting. He'd promised. They hurry past the houses, small and square like their own, keeping their eyes only on him, forgetting to watch out for the big black dog who lives a few houses up, forgetting to watch out for the boogeyman who could be anywhere.

He sees them and smiles. Then he is all arms, open, strong, gathering them up. They brush the tight drum of his cheek with their small wet mouths.

"Le fudge, Papa," they say. "On va faire du fudge à c't heure?" He laughs and puts them down. They hold his big fingers as they walk; way way up is his face.

Charles LeBlanc walked slowly, knowing it took his daughters two or three steps to match each of his. But even their exuberant welcome did not lift the heaviness that hung on him. When he saw his wife, Claire, sitting on the front steps holding André, his heart beat a little faster. Her light cotton housedress billowed gently around her legs, and her bare arms glowed rosy from the July sun. What would she say when he told her the news? Holding back his dread as if it were a small dangerous animal, he leaned over to kiss her, and patted André's downy head.

"The fudge, Daddy, when are we going to make the fudge?" chirped the two little voices by his side.

"We'll make it right after supper."

The irony of his situation struck him the most: those thousands of veterans he had found jobs for these past five years. "You've placed all that are placeable," his supervisor had told him. "You did a good job."

"Look, Daddy, I made a picture for you," Annette said, leading him inside to the child-sized table in the living-room where three or four crayon drawings lay.

"Me too, Daddy, I made one for you too," Nicole said.

For over half a century, Charles had resisted marriage. Brown-and-cream sepia photographs in the bottom drawer of his bureau showed him smiling with various women in Boston, Pittsburgh, New York and France. In some he wore his World War I soldier's uniform; in one, a broad-jawed woman with a nurse's cap perched giddily on his knee. Family life had simply not interested him then. Now, with Annette and Nicole hovering around him with their crayons and paper, he found it hard to believe he had ever felt that way.

"The mackerel man came by today," Claire called out from the kitchen. "I bought two nice big ones for supper." She leaned through the doorway to smile at him, her apron pulled snugly over the curve of her stomach. Though she was almost seven months pregnant, she still looked slim and graceful.

"Bon," he said, but he felt his uneasiness return. He had seen what happened to families when the men were out of work. If only he had been able to find something right away; then he could have told Claire he was simply changing jobs, that there was nothing to worry about. For two whole weeks, now, he'd made inquiries, studying the ads in the Halifax *Chronicle Herald* as he rode the trolley to work, jotting down places to call. But no-one seemed interested in his B.S. in Economics, in his years of experience as an engineer, manager, newspaper columnist, salesman, farmer, interpreter. He had hardly any accent—he was as comfortable in the English-speaking world as he was in the French—so that wasn't it. The shipyards and fisheries always wanted men, but only those with young bodies and strong backs. There simply weren't any positions for 57-year-old men looking for a new start in life, even one with a 33-year-old wife and young children to support.

He'd been lucky with this job. It was interesting and paid a decent salary. They had been able to move from a dark, cramped two-room apartment to this cozy four-room prefab they rented from the city. Annette had been only a tiny baby then; now she was four, and there were two more children, soon to be three more.

He looked around at the big overstuffed chair where he sat in the evenings, reading out loud from *La Vie des Saints*, Annette and Nicole perched one on each knee. Ten years ago he could not have imagined that. Who knew what to expect? Today had been his last day. He would have to tell Claire tonight.

6

When she heard his words, Claire drew her breath sharply, then hoped Charles hadn't noticed. She poked at the edges of the mackerel with her fork.

"I should have known the job would end eventually," he said. "There were only so many veterans. But don't worry; I'll find something. I've changed jobs before, after all."

This was true. He had done many interesting things. And he had travelled, seen the world. That's partly what had made him so different from the young men in the villages where she had taught, the barely literate farmhands who had followed her around like snuffling sheepdogs. She had wanted more from life than they could offer. Charles, appearing in Pomquet where she was the school principal, was like someone she had only dreamed of. When he walked with her in the evenings along the dusty country roads, his observations hummed in her ears like poems. He brought her roses.

Nicole and Annette were popping peas into their mouths, chanting softly to each other, "Papa va faire du fudge."

"What will we do?" she asked, resting the flat of her hand over her belly. "Do you have anything in mind?"

"I've been thinking of starting a small business," he said. "I have some capital and the city is booming right now. It shouldn't be hard to get something started."

She wanted to trust him completely, to know that she could rely on him. But even after five years of marriage she still found it hard to be entirely dependent on another human being. School Boards did not hire married women, so in marrying him she had given up the possibility of supporting herself. She felt a nub of fear forming: *He had known about this for two weeks and hadn't told her.*

"Du fudge," Annette and Nicole chanted. "Papa va faire du fudge." André, perched in his highchair, flung out his arm, knocking a plastic tumbler of milk onto the floor where it spread like a small river. Claire hurried to get the mop.

"Let Big Hubby do it," Charles said, leaning over her and taking the mop from her hands. This was an old affection between them. At 5' 2", she was "La Petite Femme," and he, at 6', "Le Gros Mari." He couldn't bear to see her do heavy work, preferring to do it himself. He wielded the mop carefully, thoroughly, catching up not only the spilled milk but a few muddy tracks by the back door as well. Watching him, seeing his calm, intelligent face, Claire felt her fears drain away.

After supper, while he stirred the saucepan of sugar, cocoa, and milk, Charles wondered what on earth he was going to do. He hadn't thought through the idea of a business—it was the first thing he could think of to say, to offer to Claire as reassurance. Annette and Nicole stood on chairs watching the saucepan eagerly with their big eyes. He had been many things in his life, but he had never run his own business. He needed an idea—a good idea. Something he could sell, something always in demand.

"I love fudge," Nicole said, hugging her father's arm.

"I do too," said Annette, and they did a little dance on their chairs. A pair of blue eyes, just like his, and a pair of brown eyes, just like Claire's, shone up at him.

Everyone enjoyed candy, he thought. The candy counters in all the corner groceries were always busy. He remembered being at Dan's corner store once when the wholesaler of confectionery arrived. What was it the children had called him? The Candyman. Here comes the Candyman, they'd said.

He began modestly. He bought a used half-ton truck and stocked it with penny candies: coconut balls, honeymoons, tootsie rolls, spearmint leaves, black and red liquorice twists (all of which sold for a penny each), jawbreakers (four for a penny), chocolate buds and wild cherries (three for a penny), Scotch mints, English mints and other favourites. Bub's bubble gum (the two-cent wads that came with comics), and nickel bags of Hatfield potato chips rounded out his inventory. Penny candy came in boxes roughly the size of stationery boxes; twelve to sixteen came to the carton. He bought one or two cartons of each; what he could not carry in the truck, he stored in the small shed behind the house.

With his truck so supplied, Charles set out to make his place in the city, driving from one corner grocery store to another, soliciting, cajoling, gossiping. All through the war people from rural Nova Scotia had flocked to Halifax to work in the shipyards; now that the war was over, they continued to come, drawn by the promise of prosperity. Immigrants came too: refugees from all over Europe; British fleeing their ruined homeland; even Lebanese and other non-Europeans, taking advantage of Canada's liberal immigration policies. The city was expanding westward. Clusters of houses appeared along what had once been quiet country roads; grocery stores sprang up to supply them. The hoards of children in those new settlements had prodigious appetites for candy, and Charles was the first wholesaler to come along.

Slowly, his list of regular clients grew. Though money was scarce those first few months, Claire stood by him without complaint, and it seemed that all would be well. Charles found that he enjoyed the work. His customers were so varied: the McKinnons, a Scottish couple from Antigonish County with thin mouths and pink faces; Lloyd Brown with his narrow black mustache and London accent; Paul Pettipas whose mother came from a French village not far from his own in Cape Breton. There was always something to talk about, something to observe together about the world, the economy, MacKenzie King's latest doings.

The days passed quickly. When he came home, Annette and Nicole met him, each with something to share, a story, a picture drawn at their little table, or a new song Claire had taught them. They sat on his big knees and warbled in their tiny voices:

L'as tu vue passer la chatte a grande queue,

Oui, je l'ai vue passer la semaine passee...

And always, there was Claire, eager to hear how things were going, offering encouraging remarks. In late September a country woman came to stay for a week while Claire was delivered of another son. They named him Claude after Charles' older brother, who had died of cancer a few years before.

One rainy evening in early December, five months after Charles had started his business, Claire heard the phone ring. She had just put the children to bed and thought it might be Charles, explaining why he was so late.

"There's been an accident," a strange man's voice said. "Your husband's had a heart attack. His truck hit a lamppost.

We don't know which caused which, but he's in pretty bad shape. He has several broken ribs and a fractured pelvis."

"My God!" Claire gasped.

He was still unconscious, the doctor told her, but he would probably live. Perhaps tomorrow, if he was awake, she could come to see him, but not until then.

Claire wanted to rush to the hospital, to wait in the lobby if necessary until they would let her see him. Then she remembered the children, asleep in the next room. She went into the living-room, and without turning on the light, sat in the rocking-chair. Over and over she pictured the scene—the maroon truck, light from the lamppost shimmering on the slick, shiny, treacherous road. And Charles, his straight, strong body crumpling, breaking, boxes of wild cherries and coconut balls careening past him. He had been on his way home. She rocked in the dark for a long time before she could bring herself to go into the bedroom and lie down on the empty bed.

The next day Claire was allowed a short visit. She brought the children next door to Mrs. Smith's and took the trolley to the hospital. What she saw terrified her. Charles was barely conscious, and there was so much plaster on him she hardly recognized him.

"How will you manage?" he asked her feebly.

"Don't worry about us," she said, putting her hand on his. "Just get well."

That night she barely slept, and the next morning her eyelids were swollen from crying. After breakfast, as she checked the supplies in her kitchen cupboards, Claire began to feel the full weight of their predicament. With the new baby there were now four children to feed, along with a kitchen stove hungry for coal. Christmas was coming. The old toffee tin she kept at the bottom of her hope chest contained $23.00. All the rest of their money had gone into the business.

From the window she watched a light flurry of snow swirling over the rooftops. The little prefabs seemed to shrink from it, huddling into themselves, grey and bleak. Beyond them stretched the city, the swollen English city. She had spent most of her life in French-speaking villages in rural

Nova Scotia, small communities along Saint Mary's Bay, Saint George's Bay, and the Straits of Canso where the Acadians had resettled after the Deportation. Halifax was an enormous change from village life: the downtown areas teemed with sailors, merchant marines, immigrants. Shop windows displayed all sorts of wonderful things she had seen before only in mail-order catalogues. And when she and Charles went for walks, wheeling the baby carriage through the crowds in the Public Gardens, she had tingled with excitement. With his strong arm holding hers, he had guided her through this strange, complex city, and she had come to think of it as their home. Now, even the city seemed different.

Watching the smoke curl from a chimney across the street, Claire realized that she hardly knew her neighbours. The prefabs, hurriedly constructed during the war, were intended as temporary housing, and people moved in and out of them every few months. With the neighbours she recognized, like Mr. Penny, or Mrs. Barton, Claire exchanged greetings and short remarks about the children or the weather, but that was all.

The only neighbour she spoke to regularly was Mrs. Smith next door. Mrs. Smith had been Lucille Boudreau from Belle Côte in Cape Breton before she married Earl Smith from Guysborough, who spoke no French. A few times a week Claire and Lucille stood near the borders of their yards to chat, and though their vastly different backgrounds prevented them from becoming close friends, Claire found it pleasant to have someone to speak French to besides Charles and the children.

Halifax was not at all like her real home, the village along Saint Mary's Bay, where everyone knew everyone. When there was trouble there, everyone found out about it. She remembered the October night that lightning struck their barn and burned it down. It had been a tremendous blow to her mother, a widow with five children. But Emile Comeau next door offered his barn to shelter their cow; Gustav Melanson across the road offered to house their oxen, and everyone contributed a few bales of hay to feed the animals through the winter. The following spring, all the men in the village appeared one day to rebuild the barn. Claire and her sisters helped their mother prepare huge meals for the men, and some of the wives came at meal time, bringing armloads of pies and bread. It hadn't seemed like charity at all; it had seemed more like a wonderful, two-day party.

Here, in this sea of English faces, English voices, there was no-one familiar to turn to. A picture of Charles, his body bent and broken, appeared before her. It would take months for him to recover. How would they survive without him? She felt cut loose, set adrift, like a small dory forgotten by the mother ship and left to flounder on the ocean, alone and ill-equipped. This is what came of dependence.

A light tap came from the back door. It was Lucille Smith, holding a plate of warm cinnamon rolls.

"It's not much," she said. "Just a little something for the children."

"Ah, merci!" Claire replied, touched. Lucille had four children of her own to feed and even this simple offering was generous. Lucille's husband drank up a good part of his wages; sometimes on Friday nights they could hear him when he came home, yelling at Lucille and the children in a slurred, gravelly, voice.

"Any more news about the Monsieur?" Lucille pulled her frayed sweater more tightly around her.

"No, things are the same." Lucille always referred to Charles as the Monsieur, and addressed her as Madame LeBlanc. In this, Claire recognized the enormous respect uneducated country people often had for the educated; she was careful to call Lucille "Madame Smith" in return.

"Well, if I can do anything to help, Madame LeBlanc, you let me know."

Claire watched Lucille Smith cross the yard, her thin body bent into the cold. She had lost two children; their lives had sputtered out after only a few months. Her only son, Gordie, who was a few years older than Annette, had a vacant look in his pale eyes. These and other troubles had beaten Lucille down, defeated her. The corners of her mouth pointed downward, even when she smiled, and her eyes had a wistful, yearning look.

The house felt chilly. Claire had put less coal in the stove, hoping to make the pile last two, maybe three more days. Now the wind had picked up and cold air was seeping in around the windows. What would become of them? The money in her old toffee tin would last a week or two at the most, not even until Christmas. Then what? Was she, Claire, to become like Mrs. Smith? Once she had been someone—a competent teacher, a school principal whom everyone in the community looked up to and admired. She had had ideas about life. Dreams. Now she was no-one, and her life had suddenly become small and mean. Soon, this week perhaps, or next week, she would have to pick up the phone and call someone. Someone she didn't know. She would have to ask for charity.

Christmas was grim. Mr. Penny from across the street brought over a small spruce tree, and the Fire Department supplied gifts for the children: an old truck they had repaired and repainted, a few books bearing crayon marks from their previous owners, a rag doll, some clean but worn winter jackets, a few soft gowns for the baby. Annette and Nicole didn't seem to notice the difference and filled the room with their cheerful hubbub, but when the day ended, Claire threw herself on her bed and wept.

Once or twice a week, Claire took the children to Mrs. Smith's house, and went to visit Charles at the hospital. His illness seemed huge and terrible. When it was not too cold she walked the three miles each way. With the twenty cents she saved from the trolley fare she could buy a half-pound of baloney.

Some days it seemed more than she could bear. When Nicole pointed through the window at passing trucks and said, "There's Daddy!" only sheer will kept her from falling apart. "He will be home soon," she told Nicole and herself. He will be home soon and things will be as before. She recited these words like a litany.

The brown truck from Saint Vincent de Paul and the white truck from the Red Cross made frequent stops in front of the LeBlanc house, bringing beans, bread, molasses, potatoes, puffed rice. By the back door they deposited gleaming piles of coal. With a small bucket, Claire carried the coal into the kitchen.

One windy March afternoon Nicole came in from playing and found two strange women sitting on the edges of her mother's two best chairs. They were sipping tea from her mother's treasured china cups.

"That woman just brought your father home from the hospital," her mother told her, pointing to the one dressed in white, and indicating with her tone that Nicole was to be respectful and polite. Confusing "apporter" with "porter," Nicole was convinced that the woman sitting across from her had somehow carried her huge father home—in her arms or on her back. Nicole stared at the nurse's thin arms, at her plain face and thick ankles, marvelling that such an ordinary-looking woman could have such tremendous, hidden powers. She was so caught up in wonder that for several minutes she forgot to go into the bedroom to greet her father, though she had missed him very much.

Charles had eagerly awaited this reunion with his children. But they gathered around his bed staring at him as if they didn't know him. After some coaxing, Nicole and Annette climbed on the bed and hugged him. André, however, hovered by the door gaping, his odd-coloured eyes—one green, the other brown—making him look like a furtive, exotic bird. Claude cried and clung to Claire when Charles tried to hold him.

Though he felt enormously grateful to be home, he noticed that the family tableau he had missed and longed for was no longer the same. The children had grown—little Claude, now six months old, was barely recognizable. Annette could read a handful of words, and she and Nicole could say the alphabet in both French and English. Even Claire seemed different. There was a toughness about her, a kind of fierceness he had not noticed before. No wonder, he reflected. Lord knows how she had managed during those months, with so little money and no-one to help her with the work. He pictured her mopping the linoleum floors, shovelling coal, carrying in the heavy bucket—chores he had always done for her. She had managed without him. It was as if an important balance between them had been disturbed; some harmony tilted out of sync.

When he felt well enough, he would show Claire that he could still take care of her and the children. He would pay off the debts that had accumulated during his illness, and make his business succeed. Things would return to the way they were before.

After three months without Charles, Claire was intensely aware of his returned presence in her house, in her bed. Several times a day she asked him: "Ça va? Are you all right?"

"Yes, I'm feeling much better," he told her. "Just a bit tired. I don't have all my strength back yet."

The doctors had predicted a full recovery, so Claire expected to have her old husband back. But the man who lowered himself carefully into the padded chair and fell asleep right after supper was not Le Gros Mari she remembered. There was less hair on his head, and what remained had turned almost completely grey. His flesh did not hug his bones as tightly as it once had, and his shoulders had become slightly rounded. Watching him there, quietly reading the evening paper, distant and strange, she found it hard to imagine the big handsome man she had married.

A vague disappointment, something shifting and unde-fined, nagged at her. For three long months she had been strong—for the children, for him. Now he was home, but things were not as they had been.

Still, he needed her support now, perhaps more than ever, until he got back on his feet. She brought him pillows for the small of his back, made his favourite soup. It would take a little longer than she had expected, that was all.

When he resumed his rounds, Charles found that the grocers in the outlying areas were glad to have him back. They shook his hand, listened to his stories about the accident, gave him large orders. They referred him to other stores, too, and his list of regular customers grew. Still, he found the long days tiring; his body didn't feel the same as it had before the accident.

Claire was glad to see Charles well and busy again. But though she said nothing, she noticed that he was not as atten-tive as before, and when they made love, not always successful. He seldom offered to mop the floor, and he didn't call her La Petite Femme anymore. She missed the old endearment, and mourned that small loss in a silent, private place. After all, the worst was behind them. They were gradually paying off the back rent and the hospital bills. There was plenty of food. Life was improving. Soon they would be able to start moving ahead.

As his business began to grow, Charles faced a storage problem. The four-room prefab they rented had no basement, and the small shed in the backyard was already full. Potato chips, because of their bulk, posed the biggest challenge. They came in fifty-bag cartons, and were a popular item, so he had to keep many in stock. At any given time he could carry only about twenty cartons in the truck, along with his other supplies, yet he could generally sell three times that number each week. The question, then, was where to keep the rest.

One cold drizzly day, while she was drawing at the table by the window, Nicole watched a large truck pull up in front of her house. The man who appeared at the door had a red face, big jowls, and a slit instead of a mouth. She peered out at him from behind her mother's skirt.

"Where shall I put them?" he asked.

Her father emerged from the kitchen where he had just finished his noon meal. "Bring them in here and I'll show you where to stack them," he said.

"In here?" the man asked, craning his thick neck forward. "In the living-room?"

Her mother stiffened. When the man went out to his truck to begin the unloading, her mother and father burst into words.

"Charles! Not in the living-room!"

"There's nowhere else to put them, Claire. You know the shed is full."

"But Charles, the *living*-room! What are you thinking!" Annette and André, hearing a commotion, came in from the kitchen and stood by the square brown oil stove in the corner. Little Claude crawled in behind them. The ruddy-faced man carried in four cartons of potato chips and her father directed him to stack them behind the sofa which he had pulled away from the living-room wall. The man's boots left muddy tracks on the newly waxed linoleum floor.

Claire threw herself into the armchair, convinced, now, that they would never get anywhere. They would never be anyone. They would stay forever in a crowded four-room prefab with a living-room full of potato chips. Her whole life would be nothing but work and ugliness.

As he went in and out, the man glanced at Claire weeping in the chair and made a rough attempt to wipe his feet. Four pairs of child eyes followed him back and forth across the room; the hill of boxes edged toward the ceiling.

Charles, counting the cartons as they came in, clenched his jaw. What else could he have done? Claire had always stood by him before. How could she behave like this now and in front of a stranger?

Nicole saw her mother's shoulders shaking, the hard look on her father's ashen face. Full of fear, she stroked her mother's arm and stared at her father.

2: Turf

André threw a large spruce branch onto the pile.

"Pas comme ça!" Nicole snapped. "We have to get them to stand up right."

They had spent a good part of the afternoon trying to build a camp in the backyard, dragging home branches from the woods at the end of the street. Squares of cardboard from last week's clubhouse lay in a soggy heap by the back steps. Small holes rutted the scrubby patch of yard where, a few days before, Nicole and Claude had tried to dig a hole to China with an old spoon. When Annette told them there would be hot lava and fire down there, they had quit. Annette knew things. She was in grade 2 at Edgewood School and could already read by herself. Nicole was only in primary.

"What we need now is rope," Nicole announced. "To tie them up with."

"We could use the clothesline," André suggested.

"It's too thick, dummy." Nicole said. André didn't know anything. All at once, Nicole became aware of two boys standing by the side of their house near the coal pile. Boys she didn't know.

"What do you want?" she demanded. Sometimes strangers meant a fight; other times, they meant new friends. You could never be sure. She eyed the rocks by her feet furtively. André squatted behind the branch pile.

The boys exchanged low whispers. One of them pointed to the shed and asked: "Is it true there's candy in there?"

"Why do you want to know?" Nicole cocked her head to one side, assessing them.

"Someone told us there was a shed over here full of candy, and we just want to know if it's true." He wiped his nose on an encrusted sleeve and offered a little smile.

"It's true," Nicole said, standing up a little straighter. "It's our father's."

The boys stared at the shed, their eyes round and black like jawbreakers. "Do you ever get to eat any of it?" the taller one asked.

Glancing out the kitchen window, Claire noticed the two strange boys and the defensive postures of her own children. She waited there for a moment, in case she would have to intervene. There were so many fights! At least once a week one or more of her children came tearing into the house followed by a rain of rocks. Her front and back doors bore hundreds of pockmarks from months of such skirmishes. Over and over she advocated gentleness, tolerance, peaceful living, but it seemed hopeless. With its crowded prefabs, dusty gravel roads and scrubby yards, the neighbourhood resembled a frontier town, and among the children a kind of lawlessness prevailed. They roamed through the neighbourhood in packs, scruffy and ill-kept like alley cats. Even the youngest children had a fierceness about them. Their pockets bulged with rocks, and they looked ready to fight at the smallest challenge or imagined insult.

While she might be able to control her own children, there was not much she could do about the others. She had tried shaming them, using her best school-principal voice to scold the rough-looking children who waited outside. "Don't you know you could put out someone's eye with a rock? How would you feel then?" Generally this worked for a while; then the rock-throwing gradually resumed.

Even in their own backyard, her children were not safe. She knew more of the neighbours now—many of them had lived there three or four years, almost as long as she and Charles had—but she didn't recognize these boys. Every few months families moved and were replaced. It was hard to keep track of things. At home, in the village, you knew which children to be wary of, which were likely to be a bad influence. They were the ones whose homes needed painting or whose yards were badly kept. But here, in these rented, temporary houses, it was hard to tell anything.

They were leaving now, those strange boys; she could get on with her housework. In the living-room, she straightened out the davenport slipcovers. Only one row of potato chip boxes stood against the wall behind the sofa. That meant that Charles would be getting another delivery soon. No point in waxing the floor this week, then. She had gradually reconciled herself to having the boxes there, but not without effort. At first she had draped a sheet over the pile, but found this only increased the impression of bulk. Finally, through an enormous act of will, she put them out of her mind, so that she noticed them only when the children knocked them over, or hid behind them, or made them into a fort in the middle of the room on rainy days. They were a necessary evil, she supposed, like the rough neighborhood children. Still, it was hard some days not to long for a different life, one where your efforts counted for more, where you knew you were going someplace.

When he got up at six each morning, the first thing Charles did was look out the kitchen window at the grey shed. After he felt certain that the shed had survived the night undisturbed, he poured a bucket of coal into the kitchen stove and lit the morning fire. When the kitchen felt warm and smelled of fresh coffee, he would wake Claire and the children.

This morning, as he peered through the half darkness,

something about the way the padlock hung on the shed door made him feel anxious. He pulled his pants on over his longjohns and slipped on his rubber boots. Outside, the air felt brisk and frosty. "Please, please, je t'en prie," he muttered to the handful of stars lingering in the dawn.

The lock was intact, though clearly someone had been trying to pry it open. The padlock and hasp bore shiny new scratches, and some of the surrounding wood had been chipped away by something hard and blunt, probably a rock. He circled the shed, examining other possible points of entry. The heavy plywood he had nailed over the two windows was still securely in place. After the first break-in, he had simply replaced the broken glass, assuming that the burglary had been an anomaly. After all, he had been in business a whole year by then, and the shed had not been bothered before. But that break-in had been followed by another, then another, until it seemed that all the thieves in the world wanted to get into his shed.

He looked around at the quiet little houses surrounding his own. Dim yellow lights shone from a few kitchens; smoke slowly curled from several chimneys. In one of those houses, or in one of the hundreds of houses just like them in the neighbourhood, slept the boys who had crept into his yard last night and assaulted his shed. He was sure the thieves were boys. Even before the police tracked down the two juveniles responsible for the last break-in, he had known they were boys. They always took the things boys liked—jawbreakers, black licorice pipes, bubblegum—and they rummaged around in the shed until they found what they wanted, leaving a trail of spilled candy behind them.

But which ones were the culprits this time?

There were hundreds of children in the neighbourhood, at least three or four per household. Some, like the McDonalds and the Dunfords, already had as many as eight or nine children and still produced a new baby every year. It was as if the world had been given a fresh command to reproduce and multiply, and people in the neighbourhood were doing their best to obey. At least he and Claire would not be contributing any more new lives. His accident and illness had apparently left him sterile, for there had been no pregnancies since then. For this he was quietly grateful—it was hard enough to provide for the four they had.

He thought of the neighbourhood boys again. They knew what he kept in his shed—everyone did. And while most of them were still too young to be capable of burglary, they were growing up fast. No male child older than ten was above suspicion. Gordie Smith was ten, he remembered when a light appeared in the kitchen next door. His poor mother watched him carefully, though, herding him like a dog herds sheep. Gordie was a lot like a sheep, big for his age with too pale, guileless eyes. No, it couldn't have been Gordie. But it was someone. Some boy who would try again.

Though Charles returned to the kitchen relieved that the thieves had not been successful, he felt discouraged. He had already replaced the shed's padlock once, and while this one seemed stronger, he knew that eventually it too would yield. A boy's rampage through the shed could cost him a week's profits. And there would be Claire, watching him with her big eyes, making him feel as if the burglaries were somehow his fault. Yet how could they resist, those boys? Their lives contained few luxuries, and his shed, full of forbidden pleasures, shone like a gleaming treasure house.

When he stooped to lift the coal bucket, something in his lower back rebelled. Once, he had felt invincible—he had survived the Great War, a heart attack, a serious accident. But his legs had started to ache by the end of the day, and his fingers sometimes swelled on damp mornings. He rubbed the sore spot on his back. His 60 years were catching up to him.

One afternoon, Nicole burst into the kitchen dirty-faced and sore from a hair-pulling fight. "What does it mean when you're a Frog?" she asked, massaging her scalp.

"Where did you hear that?" Claire asked.

"That's what Gloria Power called me. A stupid Frog."

Claire drew a sharp breath. She hadn't expected this kind of thing, not in a neighbourhood where there were Irish, Scots, English and French, all living together. Moreover, they were not the only Acadian family. Within a few blocks of them lived Boudreaus, Robichaus, Landrys—families who must have come from the French parts of Cape Breton or along Saint Mary's Bay, though she had never heard their children speak French. Her own children still spoke French at home, though what she heard these days had more and more English in it. The normal fights were bad enough: it would be horrible if her children had to suffer for being Acadian.

Still, Gloria Power's mother was a war bride from England, and you never knew what to expect from the English. After all, they were the ones responsible for the Great Deportation in 1755. All her life she had heard the stories: how British soldiers summoned all the men and boys over ten to the church in Grand Pré and bolted the doors behind them. Then they rounded up the women and children and put them on ships waiting in Minas Basin. In the end, thousands of Acadians were transported into exile, many to die, many never to be reunited with their families again.

Nicole was waiting for her to speak.

"It doesn't mean anything," she said. "During the war people used to call the French that just to be silly."

Nicole looked at her suspiciously. "Well, if she calls me that again, she's going to get it."

Claire watched Nicole's clenched fists, her puckered, determined face. Her sweet blond-haired, blue-eyed, angelic six-year-old daughter, transformed before her eyes into this raging, ferocious street-urchin.

"You mustn't fight. I've told you that over and over again."

"Well what can I do when she calls me names?"

Claire thought for a moment. "If you *have* to do something, you can call her a Haligonian. Then just walk away."

Nicole brightened. "What does that mean?"

"It just means someone who lives in Halifax. But she won't know that right away."

"A Hal-i-gon-i-an," Nicole repeated, pleased.

Though Nicole was satisfied, the episode left Claire feeling unsettled. The children already had enough to fight about; she hoped this would not be a portent of things to come.

When winter came, however, the fights diminished. The cold kept many children in, especially those whose parents could not provide them with warm coats. Only a scattering of children appeared around the lamppost in the evenings to play Red Rover or Simon Says. To Claire's relief, her own children seemed content to stay in after dark, quietly playing Monopoly and checkers on the floor by the oil stove. Without the influence of the neighbourhood children they seemed calmer, more like the kind of children she envisioned herself and Charles as having.

One Thursday in January, a fierce blizzard swept through the city, closing the schools and sealing everyone in under huge gusts of snow. Claire and the children watched it through the windows, swirling and leaping like something alive. Though Annette and Nicole loved school, they seemed glad to be home with André and Claude in their nice warm house. Claire made a big batch of molasses cookies and they all played snakes and ladders, and checkers for hours. Even Charles took the interruption of his routine cheerfully: he listened to a few of his opera records, played cards with the children, then took a long nap.

By the following morning the storm had passed, and the city lay buried under almost two feet of snow. Soft hills of snow heaped like ancient burial mounds hid the sheds, the cars, the fences. Charles set to work shovelling out his truck so he would be ready to go when the city ploughs passed. He could not afford another idle day. His back hurt with the effort, so he took it slowly, doing a little at a time.

The children, bundled to the teeth with only their eyes showing, ventured out into the deep, white world. They tunnelled and swam in the snow, they breathed and ate it, they threw it at each other and threw each other in it. Soon forts sprang up in the backyard. Ducky and Wayne appeared from next door. Then Sharon and Gloria from across the street. Gordie Smith, who preferred playing with younger children, joined them as well. Soon there were dozens of children, all madly hurling snowballs at each other, the boys against the girls. It was a hot, wild war that eventually raged through six yards. When the LeBlanc children came home for supper they were flushed and soaked but radiant.

On Saturday morning, four pairs of mittens and socks and

23

leggings hung on the line behind the kitchen stove; four pairs of boots huddled under the oil stove in the living-room.

"Your boots are still wet from yesterday," Claire told the children. "You'll have to wait until they're completely dry before you can go out again."

What to do? Outside, rumpled blankets of snow covered the yards, waiting; giant pillows of it lined the street where the plough had passed, inviting. Inside, the clock on the wall ticked; the four small rooms closed around them.

"Why don't you read?" Claire suggested. "Or play snakes and ladders?" Four faces looked back at her sullenly.

Late morning, the milkman arrived. When she heard the clatter of bottles, Claire went to the front door. The milkman, who had a broad smile and curly brown hair, often paused to chat with her. She looked forward to his visits; he was someone to talk to on those long days home alone with André and Claude, and the way he looked at her reminded her that she was still young and pretty.

"That was some snow we had," he said, stepping inside the front door and stomping his boots.

From the sofa, where she lay sprawled, Nicole idly observed André, who had squatted behind the easy chair. He was watching something—his green eye and brown eye were alert, like a cat's. Noticing her, he put his finger over his lips and nodded in the direction of their mother and the milkman.

"I'll need two extra quarts today," their mother said. "The children go through a lot of milk when they're home."

Nicole kept watching André. What did he have in his hand? Suddenly, a small rubber ball flew through the air and bounced off the milkman's chest. Nicole dove behind the sofa into the shelter of the potato-chip boxes.

Claire threw a dark look into the living-room, but she saw no-one, so she resumed her conversation. Behind the chair André held both hands over his mouth. His face was swollen up like a turnip and little titters exploded from his purple cheeks. The sounds drew Annette and Claude who, sensing immediately that something was up, crouched in the doorway by the hall to watch.

Nicole slipped out from behind the sofa, grabbed two of the rubber boots drying under the oil stove, and returned to her hideout. A moment later she popped up and hurled a boot at the milkman. It fell against his shoulder. His eyes and mouth popped open in surprise.

Claire turned toward the living-room, her hands on her hips, her eyes furious. "What's going on here!"

A chorus of suppressed laughter came from behind and under the furniture, but there were no children in sight. She turned to the milkman.

"I'm so sorry," she said, mortified.

But at that instant, three other boots came flying through the air and thudded against the milkman's feet. He looked around in confusion and retreated through the door, clutching his basket of empties.

Behind the armchairs, under the sofa and among the potato-chip boxes, the LeBlanc children laughed so hard they almost suffocated. Claire dragged them from their hideouts by their arms, their legs, their hair. As she released one to grab another, the loose one fled to the bedroom and scuttled under the three-quarter bed. Annette, the last one to be caught, wrenched herself from her mother's hands and joined the others under the bed. There, among the dustballs, the wadded up dirty socks and underwear, they choked and spat with laughter, their faces burning.

Claire stood at the bedroom door, furious. "Don't you *ever* do that again," she shouted to the quivering bed.

But it was too good a game to give up. Over the next few months the Simpson's delivery man was similarly treated, then the mailman, then the milkman again. An assortment of shoes and rubber boots flew through the air, propelled by invisible hands. The living-room furniture trembled with laughter.

Claire felt humiliated that her own children would behave this way. Yet no amount of scolding seemed to make a difference. She could no longer blame their antics on the bad influences of the neighbourhood children, for they had stayed indoors most of the winter. What could possibly account for this? Her eye fell on the potato-chip boxes, and she became convinced, suddenly, that they were to blame. Civilized people did not have potato-chip boxes in their living-rooms.

"How can you expect children to know how to behave when they grow up in a living-room that looks like a warehouse?" she complained to Charles at supper.

It was the old quarrel. Charles felt his face tighten. "Claire, let's not go through all this again."

"Well we have to do something. Our children are growing up like savages."

Charles stared at his plate and chewed carefully. Lord, how he hated it when she got this way! Couldn't she see that he was doing the best he could?

An easterly wind was blowing; the air smelled of fish and salt. You could get almost any kind of weather in April, Charles thought, negotiating his truck around the corner. Snow, rain, sun, fog. And you could be sure of mud. A thin drizzle fell, and the wheels of his truck squished through several mud holes that had formed in the gravel road. He was surprised to see the house all lit up; it wasn't quite dark yet.

Claire met him at the door, her brown eyes wide with excitement. She had powdered her nose and put on lipstick.

"Oh, Charles, wait till you hear."

She had cleaned the house, too, he noticed. The children's toys were neatly stacked; the linoleum floor sparkled with fresh wax. He took off his muddy boots, careful not to step off the newspaper Claire had put down, and hung up his jacket and cap. What on earth could have happened?

Claire handed him a letter. Because of an acute housing shortage, the letter explained, the city had decided to allow the hundreds of prefabs, originally intended for temporary use, to become permanent. The houses were being offered to their current tenants at a fair price with a low down-payment. The new owners would have to agree to build basements within a year, however. Tenants had a month to decide; if they declined to purchase their prefab, it would be offered to some-one else.

"It's a wonderful opportunity, Charles," Claire urged. "Our own house! It's small, but it'll be ours."

The letter had arrived in the early afternoon, after Charles had already gone back to his rounds. Claire had looked around at the small-paned windows, the plywood cupboards, the ice box, the water heater by the stove, and suddenly it had all seemed precious and beautiful, now that it might become theirs. A house and land meant permanence. Meant you were someone. That you counted. And though the house was small, and the land barely a quarter-acre, it was a start. She had scrubbed it from top to bottom in her excitement.

"It's a lot of money to come up with all at once—a down-payment and a basement," Charles said, fingering the letter thoughtfully. There was barely enough money in their savings for even the down-payment, and he had planned to put that money toward a new truck.

"We can do it!" Claire responded. "We can borrow from the credit union, and we'll economize a little more." She thought of the money she had managed to squeeze out of the household budget and hidden in her old toffee tin. She had planned to buy Easter outfits for herself and the children. They could do without them if it meant buying the house. She imagined their yard surrounded by a white picket fence. Grass instead of mud. A vegetable garden, maybe, and flowers. Certainly a rose bush. The first thing she'd plant would be a rose bush.

They ate supper quietly, deep in their own thoughts. The children crunched their fried smelts, kicked at their chairs, poked each other and then left the table to play in the living-room.

"If we had a basement, I suppose I could store my goods there," Charles said. "They'd be safe from thieves." And he could expand his inventory, too, he thought, since the basement would be much larger than the shed.

"And the children could play there when the weather is bad," Claire added. She imagined, suddenly, an end to the boot-throwing and the rock-fights, her own and all the neighbourhood children suddenly calm and well-behaved, now that there would be basements to play in.

Outside, the drizzle turned to a soft rain, a rain that would wash the coal soot off the roofs, scrub the prefabs clean. Claire and Charles listened to it fall against the windows, and across the table their hands met. As the darkness thickened around them, the little house with its future basement became for them both a sign of progress, a promise of the prosperity that had eluded them for so long.

Around the middle of May, there was a huge commotion in the neighbourhood, as trucks and tractors and crews of men moved in to construct basements.

"Don't get in their way," Claire warned her children. "Those men have work to do."

Once school was out, the Leblanc children spent their days prowling the work sites, sitting on the huge dirt piles, watching the tractors go back and forth with their big jaws full of earth and rock. One by one the little houses were raised. They perched on wooden stilts like long-legged seagulls, while crews of men worked below them, whistling and smoking and telling jokes. They worked their way up one side of a street and down the other. Swarms of children followed them like moths.

At midsummer, they arrived at the LeBlanc house.

When she woke in the morning, the first thing Nicole thought of were the crews. When she heard the drone of their talk, the chink of shovel against earth and stone below the floor of her bedroom, she threw on her clothes and rushed down to perch in a corner from which she could see everything. She loved the dank, chalky smell. Some of the men took off their shirts—their bodies gleamed with sweat. She studied the arms with tattoos.

One day, while Nicole watched a workman measure off some lengths of wood on two sawhorses, she heard him make an odd, trilling sound. It was not a whistle. It was not a hum. She had never heard anything like it before.

"Do that again," she said.

The man grinned, threw his head back and yodelled. Nicole was enchanted.

"How do you do that?"

28

The man laughed and went back to his work. But the next time he noticed her he yodelled softly, conspiratorially, watching her out of the corner of his eye.

"Show me how to do that," she asked. "Please?"

He pretended he didn't hear, put four long silver nails between his lips and began humming. She followed him around. "Please? Pretty pretty please?"

At noon, the tractors and shovels and cement trucks fell silent. After gobbling down her baloney sandwich and milk, Nicole hurried back down under the house. It smelled of earth and cigarettes and coffee. The men sat in groups, black metal lunch pails open beside them, thermos bottles steaming. Seeing her, the yodeller yodelled a bar or two, teasing. In an instant, Nicole was by his side. *"Please?"*

"It's all in the way you hold your throat and the back of your tongue," he said finally. "Here, feel this." He offered his throat.

Nicole timidly reached over. She could feel his throat muscles moving and contracting. The other workmen watched, chewing their sandwiches idly. "Now you try it," he said.

Nicole made a singing noise and bobbed her throat muscles up and down. The men laughed.

"Come here," the man said, offering her his knee. Something in her hesitated. But she edged herself on to his right leg anyway, noticing that he smelled pleasantly of earth and tobacco. He put one hand on her back and the other on her throat. "Try again," he said.

A few days later, Nicole had mastered it. She sat on her teacher's knee, slung her arm around his neck and yodelled triumphantly. The men drank their coffee, smoked, made encouraging noises.

"Nicole!" a stern voice said.

Nicole turned and saw her mother, her face white, her body huge with authority.

"Come here at once!"

The men stopped smiling and shuffled their feet. Nicole slipped off the man's knee, suddenly ashamed.

She was forbidden to go outside again until the crews had moved on. But for the next two weeks she went around the house yodelling passionately in her high, thin voice.

When the basement was finished, Charles built two rows of deep wooden shelves, one along the south wall, the other parallel to it, four feet away. Claire and the children helped him carry the penny candy from the shed to the basement shelves. The potato-chip boxes from the living-room came last, and when they were all moved, Claire pushed the sofa back against the wall for the first time in almost three years.

"The room looks so much bigger now," she said.

Nicole looked at the wide space between the sofa and the coffee table. She watched her mother moving things: the armchairs, the drop-leaf table, the plant stand with the big pink begonia. Her mother carried in a bucket and mop and plopped them down on the linoleum floor.

"Just wait till you see this room when I'm finished," she said.

From the kitchen doorway, Nicole watched her mother. Her elbows flapped like wings, and she sang out loud as she mopped. Nicole looked again at the bare wall where the boxes had been: the room seemed empty without them.

3: Plenty

On Fridays the little man comes, the dark little man with eyes that squint. *Maa—ckerel, fresh mackerel*, he sings all up and down the street. The wheels of his cart make a hollow sound, the hooves of his horse go clop-clop. *Mackerel, fresh maaackerel*! Nicole follows her mother, who joins the other mothers converging on the street, aprons flapping, change purses jingling, children fluttering around their ankles. She stares at the horse. He is enormous. His hooves are tree stumps, his teeth yellow piano keys. He swings his head and his huge nostrils snort like volcanos.

"Just look at this fish," her mother cries. "So fresh!"

They glisten on big chunks of white ice. Blue, grey-blue with silver, like the sky during a storm. The cart smells briny, like the air in Herring Cove.

"Three should be enough," she tells the man. Nicole watches the horse raise his tail: four yellow-brown piles plop out onto the street. They smell nice, like hay and mud.

"Giddyap," the man says to the horse. When everyone leaves, her mother hands her a plastic bucket and an old spoon. She points to the small piles. "For the rose bush," she says.

On Saturdays, her father comes home from Spryfield with two huge double loaves of bread still smelling warm and yeasty. Sometimes he brings a basket of peaches, or plums, or concord grapes or a whole watermelon. What will he bring today? Nicole sits on the front steps, waiting.

"Daddy, Daddy!" She runs to the truck to meet him. "What did you bring us?"

Her father carries in a big bushel basket, beaming. "I got these from a fisherman," he says. "Twelve of them for the price of two roasting hens."

Her mother claps her hands. "Lobsters!" André and Claude and Annette come running.

"We always had them while I was growing up," she says. "My brothers would go down to St Mary's Bay with a big bucket and several pairs of thick mittens. They'd put on all the mittens and reach under the big rocks. When the lobster grabbed hold, they'd pull him out and throw him in the bucket."

They all laugh at the tricked lobsters. They stare at the greenish black creatures, their claws snapping, their beady eyes watching.

"Careful," her father warns. "They'll snap your fingers off if they get a chance. Look." He takes a pencil from behind his ear and pokes it near a gaping claw. Snap. The pencil is caught, the yellow wood crushed. Claude shrieks. He wants to try. Her father finds another pencil.

"Be careful. Don't get your fingers in the way." Snap! They all shriek. Nicole wants to try. So does Annette.

"That's enough," their father says.

"Claude gets to do everything, the spoiled brat!"

"But Dad, how will you get them into the pot?" Nicole asks.

"It's easy when you know how." Her father reaches into the teeming basket and grabs a lobster by the torso, just behind the claws. "It's like picking up a kitten by the scruff of the neck," he explains. "See?" He holds the lobster up and it snaps the air. He puts it on the floor and it scuttles around, snapping furiously. Nicole shrieks, runs behind her father's legs.

The big kettle goes on the stove. Claire throws in some salt. "It's best if you cook them in sea water," she says, "but this will do." Her eyes are big. She smacks her lips.

"Watch what happens when we put them in the boiling water," their father says.

They all crowd around. In one goes. Plop. It convulses for a few seconds, then is still.

"Did you hear it?"

"What?"

"Didn't you hear it yell?"

"Charles, don't tell the children that!"

Claude starts to cry.

"Now look what you've done!"

A half-hour later they are ready. The big oak table is covered with several layers of newspaper. The forks, nutcrackers, hammer and pliers are all laid out. Her father carries in the orange-red lobsters, strangely still and awkward looking, like unwound mechanical toys. They sit at the table and bang and pick and poke and suck. Her mother makes little throaty noises. She cracks open a claw and hands Claude the pink and white meat.

4: Spoils

Charles sat in the driver's seat of the truck and pressed on the horn. He felt lethargic from the big noon meal and would just as soon have dozed in his chair a little longer, but Claire had shaken him awake, telling him it was time to get ready. Now

32

he was ready and they weren't. He had rearranged the boxes stacked behind the two passenger seats, taking care to select the hardest, least crushable types of candy to form a seating area for Annette, Nicole and André. Experience had taught him that things like spearmint leaves and wild cherries could not survive an afternoon of jostling, squirming children.

What could be keeping them? If they didn't get started soon, they would barely have time to get settled at Swan Lake before it would be time to turn around and come back. A wave of tiredness passed over him. Yesterday he'd stopped at twelve stores in Spryfield and Herring Cove and not gotten home until 6.30 PM. And Sunday, with Mass and a family outing, could hardly be called a day of rest. He thought of the little grassy spot a few yards from the small beach. If they got there soon enough, he might be able to resume his nap. He leaned on the horn again, and Annette and Nicole and André flew out the front door of the house, shouting and pushing each other.

"I get the middle!"

"I called it first in the bedroom!"

Before he could catch his breath they were all in the truck, panting and scrambling over each other in an avalanche of arms and legs.

"Watch the boxes!" he shouted. "You'll crush the boxes!"

Nicole grabbed André by the hair and tried to yank him out of his place; he squeezed her arms ferociously; Annette pushed at them both. "It's my turn to sit in the middle!" they were all yelling.

Charles felt his face redden. Why did they always have to act like a pack of wild animals? "If you don't stop fighting we're not going anywhere!" he bellowed.

Nicole let go of André's hair. André let go of Nicole's arms. Annette shuffled into the nearest seat. All three of them stared at him warily as if *he* were the wild animal. There was never a moment's peace with these children! Every Sunday it was the same—all this fighting over who would sit where. If only Claire would hurry up! He leaned on the horn again.

In a few moments Claire appeared, freshly powdered and lipsticked. She carried two large shopping-bags loaded with blankets and towels and snacks and toys, and Claude trailed along behind her, holding the edge of her skirt. She climbed into the front passenger seat next to Charles and glared at him.

"Charles LeBlanc! You expect me to get myself and four children ready in no time. And instead of coming in and helping, you sit out here and bang on the horn. Shame on you!"

Tense silence. Claire's face was white and stiff. His own felt hot and red. Annette, Nicole and André barely breathed behind him. Claude, nesting like a panda in Claire's lap, sucked his thumb loudly.

They creaked down the road at 35 miles per hour.

After a while, Claire remarked: "What a beautiful day! Look at all the wild roses in bloom!" Then Annette said, "I can hardly wait to get there!" André and Claude and Nicole stirred, making little noises of agreement. The truck hummed and sighed like a large old animal relaxing.

At Swan Lake Nicole made friends with a little red-headed girl who owned a pair of water wings.

"I wish I had a pair of water wings," she said. With water wings she could float on the surface and never have to put her feet on the slimy brown bottom where bloodsuckers lurked.

"We can take turns," the little girl suggested. For the next hour they paddled around under the eye of the giant wooden swan perched in the middle of the lake. When they decided to rest for a while and meet again later, the little girl said, "My blanket's over there," and pointed to a grey blanket where a fat red-headed woman stretched out next to a thin man in white bathing-trunks. "Where's yours?"

Nicole pointed to where her mother and father were. "Your mother's so pretty," the little girl said wistfully. Nicole examined her mother's dark hair, her slim body wrapped in a red and white flowered bathing-suit. Her mother was the most beautiful mother in the world.

"Is that your grandpa with her?" the girl asked.

Nicole thought it strange that her new friend would make such a silly mistake, and when she got back to the blanket, she gave her father a good look. She had never had a grandpa, only Grandmère and her aunts and uncles in the country. Her father lay on his side, half dozing in his sleeveless undershirt and trousers. His head, bald in the front, grey on the sides and back, rested on a plump arm, also covered with grey hair. Watching his big body moving rhythmically with his breathing, she felt a sudden surge of love for him. He was the Candyman. When he folded her in his big arms, nothing bad could happen.

Charles woke from his pleasant slumbers with the jolt of something wet and cold against his skin. A pair of blue eyes met his: "Hi Daddy," Nicole said, snuggling up against him.

Oh Lord, he thought, his irritation melting. That one. He patted her damp blond hair.

Before loading the truck the next morning, Charles examined the boxes where the children had sat. Another fight had broken out on the way home. Sure enough, a box of coconut balls had been squashed. The hard orange coating on many of the candies had cracked open, showing the chewy brown filling. "Maudit enfant bleu!" he cursed. He couldn't sell them like that. He carried in the damaged box in and placed it on a low shelf where he kept other goods he couldn't sell.

This past year he had expanded his inventory to include some seasonal novelties: chocolate Easter bunnies and eggs; wax lips and bottles with syrup; barley clear toys shaped like santas and reindeer; rainbow candy. Yet while his inventory and sales had grown, it seemed that the pile of wasted goods had grown disproportionately larger. He hadn't quite figured out the right number of seasonal things to order, so long after Easter had passed, his children were still eating perfectly good marshmallow eggs that no-one would buy.

This summer things were particularly bad. The weather was unusually hot, and some of the more fragile chocolate candy melted in the truck. Even the sturdier candy, normally stacked safely on the bottom, seemed more vulnerable, as if the heat added weight. He hadn't counted on things like this, not now, when his inventory was finally safe from thieves. But the weather, the squirming children, the vagaries of business—they were just as bad as thieves, maybe worse.

The uncomfortable feeling that he should be doing better, that he should have things more under control, nagged at him. Once he had written a column on economics for *The Saint*

F.X. Extension Bulletin. He had helped set up co-operative stores in Pictou, Antigonish and Richmond counties. He had been the expert, holding the managers accountable when things didn't go well. But things were not as simple as they had seemed, he saw now. He eyed a box of wax angels. Who would have thought that they would discolour after only a few months?

At least the damaged candy didn't go completely to waste. The children gobbled up whatever he gave them. They tormented him for potato chips, too, though those were seldom damaged, since they were stacked on top of everything else in the truck and quickly sold. Sometimes the children pestered him so relentlessly that he opened a carton just for them to eat. The 50 small bags seldom lasted more than two days. A surge of anger filled him suddenly, anger against their gluttony, against himself for giving in so easily, against life for being so hard.

He carried an armful of boxes out to his truck. A man had to keep trying though. He had to keep trying or he'd be swallowed up. He looked at his watch. Good Lord! It was already 9.30 AM and he hadn't finished loading yet.

Every morning before she went to join her friends, Nicole stopped by the low shelf in the basement to see if there was anything new. When she saw the coconut balls, she quickly filled her pockets.

When Anne Marie next door saw the coconut balls, she eagerly proposed a game of pick-up sticks on her front steps. They were on their third candy each when Barbara Barton came across the street. Nicole did not like Barbara very much. Anne Marie sometimes played with Barbara instead of her.

"What are you eating?" Barbara asked. Her mouth was small and round and she wore new barrettes in her hair.

"Coconut balls."

"Can I have one?"

"No." Nicole inched a yellow stick out from under the pile.

Barbara watched silently for a while, then said: "I love coconut balls."

"Too bad."

"What if I pay you for some?" Barbara rooted in her pocket and pulled out three pennies. Barbara always had spending money and regularly came back from Dan's store with popsicles and comicbooks. This was one of the things Nicole disliked about her.

"Well, okay." She thought of the three cents she had hidden in her shoe. For six cents she could buy herself a root-beer popsicle. She handed Barbara three coconut balls.

Barbara looked at them and sneered. "Heck, I can get three for three cents at Dan's—good ones, too, not squashed. Why should I buy these ones from you?"

"Okay, okay," Nicole replied. It had been a long time since she'd had a root-beer popsicle. "What if I give you three more? That's two for one cent."

Barbara quickly forked over her three pennies.

A few days later, when Nicole came home with a brand new Little Lulu comicbook, Claire questioned her.

"Where did you get the money to buy that?"

"From Barbara and Gloria," Nicole said.

"You mean they gave it to you, just like that?"

"Not exactly...."

"What do you mean not exactly?"

"Well, I gave them some of Dad's old candy. The stuff he lets us eat." She looked up at her mother with clear blue eyes. "That wasn't bad, was it?"

Claire hesitated for a moment. "No, dear, it wasn't bad." Later that afternoon, Claire went down to the basement to see for herself. On the shelf in the corner she found six boxes of damaged goods. The number astounded her. Even at the pre-wholesale prices Charles paid, six boxes represented a sizable sum. She could feed the family for several days on that, or buy some new dishes, or replace the lamp André had broken.

She thought of all the scrimping and careful managing she did to keep the children properly clothed and fed. Yet their lives were not improving. Though they would eventually own the house—the monthly payments were the same as the old rent—nothing else was changing. They were standing still, while others in the neighbourhood sped on around them. Mrs. McKinnon a few doors down, whose husband was a Fullerbrush man, put a new coat on each of her children every fall while her own had to have hand-me-downs. Mrs. Barton across the street, whose husband was a foreman at the shipyards, had just bought herself a new sofa with matching easy chairs; Claire, making pillow-cases out of flour sacking at the table in front of the window, had watched the Simpson's delivery man carry them in.

And all this waste!

She picked up a handful of liquorice babies flattened together into a mass and pulled them apart with her fingers. Though they were a little crushed, they were certainly not unappetizing. And these discoloured chocolate buds—she popped one into her mouth—they tasted fine. Even the broken wax lips—someone might want them if the price were right. An idea began to form, a small hopeful path that might lead somewhere. Salvaging what she could, Claire went upstairs carrying four boxes.

"What are you doing, Mom?" André and Claude looked up from the Lincoln logs spread out on the floor around them.

"Wait till you see," she said. "Bring that little table over here by the door."

She gathered the children around her. "Now listen: I want you to tell everyone you know that they can buy good candy, real cheap, at our front door. And tell them to tell their friends."

They came in trickles at first, children with their pennies and nickels, not quite believing.

"Are you really selling candy here, Mrs. LeBlanc?"

"Yes," she said, showing them the table. "It's half-price."

Their eyes grew big. They could hardly believe their good fortune. Claire recognized a few of her customers as the rock-throwing ruffians she had scolded a few times. Their hands—chubby, mostly dirty children's hands—and their eager, hopeful faces touched her. She saw in them a portent of her own future—a future where anything could happen, where unexpected bounty waited to astound.

By the end of summer, Claire was doing a booming business. Not only children, but adults knocked at her front door, sometimes coming from several blocks away. Even Mrs.

Barton, with all her airs, could not resist a bargain, Claire noticed. She regularly sent Barbara over to buy things for the whole family. Claire's own children were now forbidden to eat all they wanted of the damaged goods; Claire allowed them only a piece or two of something every day. With candy that looked truly unappetizing, like the oozing wild cherries or the melted sponge toffee, she was more generous. When the supply of damaged boxes dwindled, she opened up new boxes and sold the candy for the same low price. Since Charles bought the candy for less than wholesale, they could still net a significant profit.

"You're so smart," Lucille Smith said to Claire one day over the back fence. "To sell the candy like that."

Claire hardly ever saw Lucille anymore except occasionally on Monday mornings when they both hung out the wash. And though they still called each other Madame, they now spoke to each other mostly in English.

"It keeps me busy," Claire said. "And I couldn't stand to see it all go to waste."

Claire didn't tell Lucille that times were hard for them, and that's why she had started her business; Lucille's need was so much greater than theirs. She and her husband had managed the down payment to buy their prefab, but Mr. Smith's drinking bouts had become more frequent and money more scarce. Last winter Lucille had taken a job in the laundry at the Halifax Infirmary. She worked all night and slept while her children were in school. When summer came, and her children were at home, she slept only in snatches, a few hours here and there. Now she looked even more haggard than ever; her thin shoulders hunched forward as if to ward off blows.

"And how are things with you, Madame Smith?"

"Oh, the same. Things will get better after next week when school starts. Then I can sleep a little." She smiled her sad smile, the corners of her mouth tilting down.

Mrs. Smith's two oldest children, Doreen and Gordie, were both in the auxilliary class at Saint Agnes School. Doreen, at thirteen, was an attractive girl who looked normal, but had difficulty learning. Gordie, at eleven, still could not read a simple sentence.

39

Thank God my own children are bright, Claire thought. That would be the worse thing. Worse than anything else.

"And how's the Monsieur?" Lucille asked.

"He's fine."

"He works so hard." Lucille sighed. "You're lucky to have a good man like that."

Throughout the fall, Charles observed Claire's activities with a mixture of admiration and discomfort. At first he had thought her clever. The day he came home and saw the little table, Claire had looked excited and happy, with an attractive flush in her face. But what had started as a minor diversion had now become a full-blown business. He felt an uneasiness, as if some established order were tilting dangerously askew.

One Sunday in October, while they were on their way to church, a little girl nudged her mother's elbow and gestured toward Claire. "That's the lady who sells candy," she said. Charles felt embarrassed—stung, almost. A man was expected to provide for his family. After that, when he met people from the neighbourhood, he sometimes found it hard to meet their eyes.

The week before Halloween, business became particularly demanding. Shopkeepers bought large quantities of candy corn and molasses kisses, and Charles was glad that he had stocked plenty of these seasonal items. Most days he had to come home once or twice to load up again. Business would be slow for a few weeks after Halloween, so he knew he had to make up for it now.

Traffic at his front door was also heavy. People were taking advantage of Claire's low prices to prepare for the hundreds of trick-or-treaters who would soon swarm through the neighbourhood. Charles was tired after the long days on his rounds, but he found it hard to relax because of the constant knocking, the draught from the opened door, the commotion. One evening he told Claire: "You don't have to do this, you know. We can manage without it. Business is very good right now."

Claire, who had spent a large part of the afternoon answering the front door and running up and down the basement stairs to replenish her supplies, stared at him.

40

"You should be glad I'm doing something to help out," she said. "Look at all the things I've bought with the money—the lamp by your big chair, the wall clock, the little end tables."

She almost added, *things we wouldn't otherwise have*, but held her tongue. It wasn't his fault when business was poor or candy got spoiled. Still, she had begun to notice that he was sometimes careless and didn't always use his time well, coming home for things he had forgotten, or not loaded enough of in the first place.

"But it's so much work for you," he countered, remembering a time when Claire was happy to leave most of the heavy work to him. She was softer then, had looked up to him.

"I *enjoy* doing it," Claire insisted.

In fact, Claire couldn't remember when she had last enjoyed herself so much. She revelled in the exchange of smiles, the friendly greetings, seeing people leave content. And though the running back and forth to answer the door sometimes left her exhausted, she felt part of a larger world now, a world where things happened, where a person could get ahead.

Most of all, she enjoyed seeing her old toffee tin fill with money. With every knock at the door, every coin that clanged into the tin she felt that their lives were improving. She had grand plans, too: she was saving for something really special the whole family would enjoy, something she would surprise them with. She couldn't stop now.

"I can manage, Charles," she assured him.

The neighbourhood grocers, however, did not take this intrusion into their territory lightly. They took note of their dwindling candy sales and investigated. Over the winter months, Mr. Robertson from Johnny's called twice to complain.

"You're taking away all our candy business," he told Claire. "That's not fair."

"I've as much right to sell candy as anyone else," Claire answered sweetly. Since they did not buy their candy from Charles, their protests seemed irrelevant to her.

One day in May, ten months after Claire had begun her business, a nice-looking man with a little blond moustache appeared at the front door. At first Claire thought he was a customer and greeted him with a bright, cheerful face. He identified himself as a city inspector.

"We've had complaints," he told her. "The area isn't zoned for commercial activity. I'm afraid you'll have to close your business."

Claire felt her mouth fall open in surprise.

"But we aren't hurting anyone or causing any trouble! There's no public nuisance. In fact we're doing a service to the neighbourhood!"

"I'm sorry," the man said, smiling apologetically. "If it were up to me..." He shrugged his shoulders and looked at her sympathetically.

Numbed, Claire watched him walk up the street. All winter she had done a brisk business, even with the cold weather. The month before, she had emptied the money tin to buy her special surprise—a new radio-record player console to replace the old tinny portable. Her eyes fell on its polished wood surface. How the children loved it! Evenings, they spread themselves out on the floor and played their Sleeping Beauty and Cinderella records over and over again. Even the news sounded more important told in the new radio's rich sonorous tones.

She had planned to buy a new oil stove at the end of the summer to replace the dirty coal stove; now she would have to do without it. There would be no more money in her money tin, no more improvements. Things would return to what they had been and she would have to rely on Charles for everything. With a rush of anger she closed the candy boxes, dismantled the display table.

"It's all the fault of those selfish neighbourhood grocers," she railed to the family at supper. "Mr. Robinson and probably Dan, too—who else would have complained! Well I can tell you, they'll never have *my* business again, that's for sure. Even if I have to go all the way to Oxford Street to buy groceries!"

The children ate their soup quietly, watching their mother. They had never seen her cheeks so flushed, her eyes so wild.

When a knock came at the front door they all stopped eating.

"It's probably somebody to buy some candy," Annette said in a small voice.

"Go and tell them that the selfish neighbourhood grocers have put a stop to that," Claire said, blazing. "Ask them what they think of that!"

"Now, Claire..." Charles began. He felt sorry for her, for her anger and disappointment, for what this had meant to her. He felt vaguely guilty, too, as if his own ambivalence toward her efforts had caused them to fail. He wanted to reassure her that things would be all right, that they would manage, but the look she gave him made him fall silent.

A few weeks later, Claire found herself with nothing to cook for supper, and reluctantly sent Nicole to Dan's for a pound of baloney.

Anne Marie, who had been sitting on her front steps when Nicole passed, agreed to walk with her. When they arrived, they found a handful of children bending in front of the glass case where Dan displayed the penny candy, pointing and jostling each other, arguing over what they should buy. Dan stood behind the counter, drumming his fingers against the glass case.

"Hurry up and make up your mind," he said. "I haven't got all day." His eyebrows, thick and black, almost met over his nose.

When it was her turn, Nicole handed him two quarters and said in a small voice, "I need a pound of baloney." Secretly she was afraid of Dan. He was big and dark, like the black bear they kept on a chain in Waverly, where her father sometimes took them on their Sunday drives. Even his voice sounded like a growl.

"He's so mean," Anne Marie whispered when Dan went over to the meat case. "He's always mean to kids."

Nicole recalled the chant they often sang a safe distance from the store:

Dan, Dan, the dirty old man,
washed his face in a frying pan,
combed his hair with the leg of a chair,
died with a toothache in his ear.

Thinking of it made her feel a little better.

They watched Dan take out a fat tube of pink baloney and saw off a dozen thin slices. He wrapped them in white paper, tied them with a string, then leaned over the counter and peered at Nicole with his black eyes.

"What's your name, little girl?"

"Nicole LeBlanc," she replied, convinced that he had read her thoughts and she was in big trouble.

"You're the Candyman's daughter, aren't you?" "Yes," she replied, astounded.

"I've seen him around," Dan said nodding.

On the way home, Anne Marie started chanting Dan, Dan, the dirty old man... But Nicole didn't join in. She was thinking that maybe Dan wasn't as bad as everyone thought. After all, he knew who she was.

5: The Rented House

Claire stepped down from the truck and took a deep breath. The air was fragrant, salty. Beyond the fields across the street the silver blue of St. Mary's Bay shimmered against the sky. The children were unfolding themselves from the long ride, blinking and dazed, as if they had just emerged from a dark tunnel.

It had taken them six hours to drive the 170 miles from Halifax, stopping as they did in Windsor and Kentville and Annapolis Royal for lunch and gas and snacks and to let the children go to the bathroom. But now they were here.

She scanned the familiar white house where she had spent the first eighteen years of her life. Her brother Louie and his wife Yolande appeared at the door; her mother, smaller and frailer than ever, followed close behind. Soon everyone was hugging and the dogs were barking and all the little cousins were grinning shyly at each other.

"T'as pas changé—belle comme toujours!" Louie said. He was short and stout, with a good-natured twinkle in his eyes. Though he was 46 and balding, Claire still saw the big brother, who at thirteen, had suddenly become the man of the family.

She was only five when their father died, and because she was the youngest, Louie had always kept a special eye out for her.

"Charles, ça va bien?" He thumped Charles on the back.

It thrilled her to hear French again. Some part of her that lay hidden, dormant, in the English world bloomed here, in this Acadian village, awakened by the sounds of her childhood language. In that other world, in Halifax, she took for granted the strangeness that always shimmered around events, the way people did things, the rough, angular way they pronounced her family's names. But each summer, when she returned here, when she felt this rush of recognition, of connectedness, she also felt the dissonance, the strain, of her life among the English-speaking.

Listening, now, to the warm, lilting cadences of her brother's voice, her mother's, then her own and Charles' responding, she felt herself uncoiling. She had faced the summer discouraged, demoralized by the closing of her small business, by the constant struggle to get by, by life itself. A good visit here, among her own people, where she was understood and accepted, was exactly what she needed.

This visit, moreover, would be an extra-special one. Normally, Charles stayed for two or three days then returned to Halifax; at the end of the following week, he came to collect them. But this year she and the children would stay for a whole month. A month of lobsters pulled out from under the rocks at low tide, of clams dug by the bushel from the soft wet sand along the bay, of long pans of pâté a la râpure and fresh blueberry pies.

It would be good for the children, too, she thought, nudging André forward. He always behaved shyly when they first came, peeking out at his cousins from behind her legs.

"Viens, un gros gars comme toi!" Yolande said.

"Your aunt thinks you're too big for this," Claire said, then repeated herself in French. They needed to hear it, to speak it again, to remember they were Acadians. Though she and Charles still spoke French to one another occasionally, they spoke mostly English to the children. It seemed easier, somehow, surrounded as they were by English voices. Still, she wanted the children to know about their Acadian heritage, to take pride in it. She had told them about the Expulsion of the Acadians, about Evangeline and Gabriel, but that was not enough. They needed to seep themselves in Acadian culture, renew their roots. Now, for a whole month, they would be able to.

And for once, they would all be under the same roof. Annette and Nicole would no longer have to sleep at her sister Isabelle's house a half-mile down the road; André and Claude would not have to take their meals across the street with her brother Roland's family. This summer they would have their own house.

After supper, they all went to look at it. It stood on the highway half way between Louie's house and Isabelle's, which was why Claire had noticed its shuttered windows the summer before. Like many other country people, the owners had gone to Halifax to find work and lived in rented rooms there. They got home as often as they could, they told Claire when she contacted them, but that wasn't more than a few times a year. And yes, they would be happy to rent the house, they said, gladly accepting the $20.00 she offered.

"It doesn't have indoor plumbing," Isabelle said, joining them on the front porch.

Claire had hardly expected indoor plumbing, since there were only three indoor toilets in the whole village. But Isabelle had one of them, and took great pride in it. Hebert had installed it himself behind a curtain in their bedroom. Isabelle, like Claire, had gone to normal school in Truro, then taught for several years in various parts of the province before marrying Hebert, who came from "down home." Isabelle's toilet and kitchen faucets set her apart from the other country women, who were less educated and had never been anywhere.

The rented house did have electricity, and when they flicked on the switch in the living-room, it became clear that the house had not been lived in for some time. Cobwebs draped like lace doilies from almost every corner, some of which were guarded by ferocious looking spiders.

"Do they bite?" Claude asked, hanging on to Claire's leg. Tante Yolande, wearing her habitual apron, had brought her broom and set to work sweeping them away.

46

On the first floor, three rooms opened into each other: a living-room, dining-room and large kitchen. A huge brown horsehair sofa and two matching easy chairs dominated the living room; the dining-room was empty, but a large round table and three wooden chairs stood in the middle of the kitchen.

"We can lend you a few more chairs, and whatever else you need," Isabelle said.

Louie primed the pump and a thick, stinking rush of brown water rumbled out.

"It'll be all right after it gets going," he assured them, and to prove it, he kept pumping until the water ran clear.

How eager they all were to help out, to make sure that she and the children would be comfortable, Claire thought, touched. They always treated her like a visiting dignitary, almost like they would the Monseigneur.

Upstairs they found three bedrooms, each with a double bed, two with dressers, and when they threw open the shutters, the rooms, though dusty, filled with light and air. In the back bedroom, long green fingers of ivy reached through a broken pane of glass and climbed part way down one wall.

"It isn't fancy," Claire remarked to the small army following and awaiting her judgment. "But we'll be fine, here."

The outhouse was another matter. The door didn't quite close, and the whole area stank.

"It could use a little lime," Louie laughed. "We'll bring some over later." Claire knew that he would not go to bed that night until he had thoroughly limed the outhouse for them. Tomorrow he would probably come and plane the door.

Nicole didn't mind the outhouse at all. She liked it much better than the toilet at Tante Isabelle's, where only a curtain hid her, and where at night, she could feel her aunt and uncle listening from their bed while she peed. She preferred it to the outhouse at Tante Yolande's, too. There, the outhouse was attached to the little shelter for the pig, and sometimes while she sat there doing her business, the pig would stick his ugly snout through the slats and grunt at her, scaring her half to death. To avoid the pig, she sometimes squatted behind the barn when no-one was looking.

Later, while her mother and father talked in the kitchen, Nicole went into the living-room and stretched herself out on the huge horsehair sofa. She fastened her eyes on the ceiling light. Surrounding the bulb were little pieces of glass, delicately carved into upside-down exclamation points. When André slammed the front door they all shook. Light tinkled off them like little bells, filling the room with tiny dancing rainbows. It was the most beautiful thing she had ever seen.

When Nicole got up the next morning she found her mother and father and Claude at the kitchen table finishing breakfast. When Claude saw her, he gobbled down what remained in his bowl.

"What are you eating?"

"They're all gone," Claude said, looking triumphant.

"What's all gone?"

"There were only a few," her mother reassured her. "Yolande brought over some blueberries a little while ago. But don't worry, we'll pick a whole bucket today and you can eat all you want."

Her mother and father seemed different today. Her father held a mug of coffee in his hands and leaned on the table. At home her father always ate his breakfast before they got up, then rushed around doing things.

She ate some cereal, without blueberries, and since Annette and André were still sleeping, said to Claude: "Let's go look at Uncle Louie's barn."

On their way, they stopped at the house to see if Pierre, Jean Paul and Antoine had started their chores yet. The most delicious smells were coming from Tante Yolande's kitchen. Last night, just before supper, Nicole had crept into the pantry and seen a gingerbread, three pies, and two twin loaves of bread, shiny and plump like babies' bums. Between the two families, they had eaten two pies and a whole loaf of bread in one sitting. Now Tante Yolande was making something else. Her big upper arms shook while her strong hands thumped and kneaded the dough. Nicole wondered if the gingerbread were still on the shelf. How nice it would be if Tante Yolande would offer them a piece.

48

"Bonjour! Avez vous bien dormi?"

Nicole nodded her head yes, they had slept well. She wanted to ask about the gingerbread, but couldn't remember the right words. Last night at supper, she had listened hard while all the grownups talked. The words had sounded vaguely familiar, like an old dream she remembered bits and pieces of. But she couldn't quite make them work in her own mouth yet. They were like little birds, those French words. Little birds that flew through the air, singing.

The kitchen door opened and Jean Paul came in carrying a huge bucket of milk. There were always two buckets, so that meant Oncle Louie was still milking. Nicole rushed out to the barn and, sure enough, on a little three-legged stool, sat her uncle, pulling at the cow's milk sac. Streams of steamy milk thrummed into the pail. She thought of Heidi, who milked goats in the mountains. If only she could learn how to do it, too. "Viens!" Oncle Louie gestured that she should come closer. She took a few timid steps. The cow's huge flanks and swishing tail made her a bit nervous.

"Viens!" Oncle Louie urged her again.

Suddenly a warm frothy liquid squirted into her face. Through her shock and discomfort she heard her uncle laughing. An old trick: he did this to her at the start of every visit. Why had she not remembered? Grinning and pleased with himself, Louie handed her the towel draped over his shoulder. Nicole roughly wiped the milk from her face.

"He really got you that time," came a voice.

It was Claude, standing in the doorway, holding a chunk of gingerbread.

"How did you get that?"

"Tante Yolande gave it to me."

Nicole threw down the towel and rushed back to the house. But the kitchen was empty; Tante Yolande and the gingerbread were nowhere in sight.

Charles had always enjoyed the short annual respite from his noisy brood; it gave him a chance to catch up on his paperwork, nap in the evenings and listen to the classical music station without interruption. This year he would have four whole weeks of peace and quiet.

After his rounds, he prepared himself a simple supper of canned stew and sliced bread. The evenings were still warm, hot even; the change wouldn't come until the middle of August. He opened the inside door to let the air circulate a little through the screens and settled in his easy chair under the lamp. Beside him on the floor lay a small pile of books he had taken from the glass bookcase. When he picked up his old copy of Spencer's *Principles* he felt as if he were rediscovering a lost friend. Once he had read a great deal. In the old days in Pittsburgh and Boston, he would buy one or two books a month and read them studiously. He had kept up with the latest in social and economic theory then; and even later, when he returned to Nova Scotia, he still bought and read books. Now the money went for other things. Except for these short periods when Claire and the children were away, there was no time to read anyhow.

He had treated himself to a Sunday *New York Times*, a few days old now, but with much still to be read. Two decades before, he had felt his Sunday incomplete without reading the *Times*. Now, it was like peering into a familiar but distant world. He picked up the paper and turned again to the editorial section. That fellow McCarthy continued to accuse the US Congress of being infiltrated by communists. How amazing that anyone would take him seriously! He thought of the fishermen around Antigonish Harbour, practically robbed of their goods by middle-men and half-starving until the co-operative movement got started among them. He thought of how he had praised the co-operatives in his column, helped set up a number of them. He snorted under his breath. McCarthy would probably have thought they were all a bunch of communists.

The world was a complex, interesting place. And a man's struggle to find his place in it, to live and provide for his family, was long and hard. He felt privileged sitting in his chair thinking about it all, as if his thoughts could put an order on all that chaos, as if figuring it out gave him some power over it. It was like the old days.

One night, toward the end of his second week alone, Charles woke to the high-pitched whine of one of the children calling for a drink of water. Out of long habit he began slipping out of bed. Then he noticed that Claire was not beside him and remembered. He listened to the darkness, thick and close around him. One of the cats yowled under the window.

He put on his slippers and shuffled to the back door. After a little coaxing, Solomon appeared, darting looks over his shoulder like a fugitive. Charles stroked the cat's ears. He had found him in Spryfield one day, a scrawny, flea-ridden kitten with open sores around his neck, and brought him home. Now he was a burly, well-fed tom.

"Up to no good, were you?"

The cat purred and rubbed up against him. He lifted Solomon gently and carried him to the basement stairs. Before returning to bed he stopped by the children's room and looked in. The shades were up and there was enough light from the lamppost to see the flat shape of the empty beds. The sight pierced him. The room, so tidy, so silent. Suddenly, he wanted Claire and the children back. He wanted their noise and hubbub, their laughter, the way they filled the house. The thought of two and a half more weeks without them seemed, at that instant, more than he could bear.

He went back to bed, telling himself not to be foolish. Claire and the children flourished in the country, and he had his books, his newspapers, his thoughts about life and the world.

But after that night, everything changed. Where once the evenings had felt peaceful, they now seemed endless and boring. When he read, the words blurred on the page and he found himself remembering the way André sat on his lap begging for stories, the way Nicole held her cheek against his when it was time to say goodnight. When the shopkeepers asked him, How's the Missus, he felt bereft, abandoned.

He wrote Claire a long letter, telling her how glad he was that she had married him, how in their ten years together he had discovered what life was really all about. He called her "Ma Petite Mignonne," a term of endearment he had used during their courtship. Finally, he asked her to come home.

Claire watched Annette and Nicole tiptoe along the water's edge. André and Claude were busy making a sand fort with Denni and Guillaume, Isabelle's boys. The tide was on its way out, so she wouldn't have to worry about the children for a while. When it came in, it came in a great rush and licked at their ankles as they retreated. Though these tides were tame compared to those farther along the Bay of Fundy, there was still danger in being caught unaware.

She had tucked the letter among the towels and sweaters and underwear she had brought for this outing, and now that the children were occupied, she took it out to read again. The ardent tone of the letter surprised her. She and Charles always exchanged a letter or two during these annual separations—chatty letters, hers full of what the children were up to, his describing the weather, business, the cats' antics. He closed his letters saying that he missed her and would be glad to have her back—but that was nothing compared to this.

She glanced over at the boys, who were shrieking with pleasure. André had just dug up a huge clam. André. For the first three days here, he had not spoken a single word to any of the relatives, and when one of them spoke to him, he lowered his head. Now, after two and a half weeks, he laughed and played and talked with his cousins, and in French. They had all caught on fairly quickly. She spoke French almost exclusively to them now, though the children still sometimes responded in English. What a pity it would be to leave now, when things were going so well!

Still, Charles' words stirred her, reminded her of the early days, before the accident, before the children. She got up to walk along the shore. A huge field of Queen Anne's lace, wild chicory and brown-eyed susans stretched back behind the strip of marsh. She had walked in such a field once with Charles, in Pomquet. They had brought a picnic lunch, and lounging on an old quilt, they had planned a future together. She remembered the poem she had written about that day:

Your love was mine in Columbine,
In beds of Phlox and Goldilocks;
Among cowslips I kissed your lips—
It was divine in Columbine.

52

Ten years had passed. Could they feel that way again?

Annette came running toward her with a handful of seashells, wanting to know what kind of creatures had lived in them. The sea with its exotic, turbulent life fascinated her. Already her collection of shells and sea mosses occupied a whole corner of the rented house. Back in Halifax, the children would have nothing to do but hang around the neighbourhood, subject to who knew what kind of influences.

She would write to Charles tonight, tell him that she just couldn't pick up and leave halfway through the month; her family might think she had been unhappy, or had found them inhospitable.

Only a little longer, she would say, then we'll all be together again. She would sign it "La Petite Femme."

But Charles' next letter, more ardent than the first, begged her to come home.

Claire had not yet decided on a response when Gustav, a boy from down the road, burst into Louie and Yolande's kitchen one evening looking for her. Roland and Elise had come, too, for an evening's conversation. She was wanted on the phone at the General Store, Gustav told Claire, a call from Halifax.

Immediately Claire imagined a truck smashed against a lamppost, Charles' ruined body lying by its side. But Gustav said: "It's the Monsieur himself who is calling."

When Claire got back, she announced that Charles was coming that weekend, and that she and the children would be returning to Halifax with him. Louie's face lit up with a mischievous grin.

"A month is a long time for a man to be without a wife," he said to his brother, Roland. "Poor devil, you can't blame him."

"No," answered Roland, winking. "Imagine having no-one to do your washing and cooking for that long. It must be hard on him."

"Oh, shoo!" Elise said, cuffing her husband's shoulder. But they all laughed, and Claire felt her face turn pleasantly pink.

Charles rushed through his rounds and left right after. Without all the stops that Claire and the children required, he was able to get there in only four and a half hours. Though he was exhausted when he arrived at 9.30 PM, he was smiling and exuberant.

The children lay awake, waiting for him. He cuddled them in their beds, holding their small, warm bodies, smelling their fragrant children's smell. The weather had turned a few days before, putting a chill on the evenings, and Claire had made a fire in the kitchen stove. She had baked him a blueberry pie, too; it sat on the kitchen table, round and inviting. When he came back down, he found she had laid the table and cut two big pieces. She had put on fresh lipstick, too, and her eyes were soft and shining.

On the way home the next day, dark clouds hung in the sky and the air smelled of rain. The children were moody and quarrelsome. When they stopped in Annapolis for dinner, Claude spilled his milk and André complained that there was nothing good to eat. Large black flies in the restaurant buzzed around their food, making it an altogether unpleasant meal.

Twenty miles down the road, Claire discovered a salt shaker in Claude's hand.

"We'll have to bring it back," she said.

"But Claire, that will cost us at least an hour!"

"Charles, it's not ours, after all."

The children in the back seat were watching him. What would he do? Reluctantly, he pulled over and turned the truck around.

After that, the trip seemed to take forever. Every half-hour or so, one of the children asked, "How much longer till we get there?" Several fights broke out in the back seat.

By the time they arrived home, Charles had forgotten why he had wanted them all back so soon. Within minutes of their arrival, the house filled with clutter: suitcases to be unpacked, sacks of odds and ends brought along to pass the time, souvenirs, Annette's shell and moss collection. And noise. So much noise!

Claire assembled a makeshift meal of whatever she could find in cans. The children hurried through their supper, then rushed to the radio in the living-room to listen to Amos and Andy, and Boston Blackie—shows they had not heard in three weeks. Claire looked across the table at Charles. Now that

54

they were alone, she hoped he would say something sweet, tell her how nice it was to have her home. But he seemed not to be thinking of her at all. He just kept eating. When he finished, he said, "I have some work to do," and disappeared into the basement.

Sitting by herself, surrounded by the debris of the meal, Claire thought of the rented house—the quiet evenings, the pleasant visits with her relatives. They could have stayed another week.

6: Fevers

School would be starting soon. The LeBlanc children hung around the back steps, restless.

"I'm going to get a new pencil-case," Nicole said. "Mom said we could each pick out a new set of pencils, too," Annette added.

"Me, too," Claude chimed.

"Claude, you're not even in school yet." Nicole said.

"I am too, I am too."

"You have to be five by the *first* of September, dummy. You won't be five till the *middle* of September."

"Mom said I could get some pencils, anyway."

Nicole glared at her brother, at his eager little face, his little rabbit teeth. It seemed to her, suddenly, that he always got everything, just because he was the baby. The whole time they were in the country, everyone had petted him—Tante Yolande with her cakes, Oncle Hebert letting him ride on the wagon while the others had to help gather the hay.

"You're just a spoiled brat," she said and gave him a shove.

He pushed back and a scuffle broke out. Nicole gave him a good kick in the stomach, and Claude went into the house crying at the top of his lungs. Instantly, she regretted having kicked him so hard, but she felt André and Annette watching her.

"It serves him right," she muttered, so they would see she was not to be tangled with.

The next day Claude did not feel well. He hung around his

55

mother and wanted her to hold him on her lap. He felt warm and complained of a pain in his stomach. By early afternoon, Claire realized that something was seriously wrong.

"I have to take Claude to the hospital," she told the other children. "Go next door to Mrs. Smith's until I come back."

In the taxi on the way, Claire felt heavy with foreboding. Claude had always been a happy child, calm and sweet-natured. He seldom complained about things, and the fact that he did now made her afraid. She held his warm limp body on her lap, and he leaned into her.

In the examination-room, the nurse began to undress him gently. Limp and pale, he hung onto his underpants, not wanting this strange woman to see his nakedness.

The sight of this pierced Claire's heart.

"Does he have to take them off?" she asked the nurse.

"I'm afraid so," she said, and pulled his little hands away.

He whimpered, defeated, and Claire felt a wave of nausea pass through her.

The doctor said, "We don't know what's wrong yet. It might be appendicitis. We'll need your permission to operate if it's necessary."

"Mon Dieu, Mon Dieu," Claire whispered to herself, swaying slightly. She had nursed her children, soothed their tears, carried them through their fights and falls and measles. But against this, she was powerless. She felt her legs turn rubbery.

She would have to leave now, the nurse told her. Parents were not permitted to stay. She could come back the next day during visiting hours.

Claire watched the nurse's mouth, an English mouth, move up and down. They were making her leave her child, alone and frightened among strangers. They would cut open his little white body, his perfect little belly... Her head spun, her own stomach lurched. Nothing in her life had ever felt like this.

On the way home, the taxi driver had to stop twice so Claire could throw up by the side of the road.

When she got home, Charles met her at the door.

"What happened? When I got home a little while ago the children came running from next door saying that Claude was sick."

"Oh Charles!" she said and collapsed against him. The children stared at her, their eyes huge with fear.

That evening, they said the rosary three times. Annette, Nicole and André knelt against the sofa, Claire and Charles by the two easy chairs. "Je vous salut Marie, Mere de Dieu..." None of the children complained; their faces were sober, silent.

Claire barely slept that night. Twice, Charles got up and found her sitting in the kitchen.

"You need to sleep," he said, and led her back to bed. "Dr. McLean will take care of Claude. He'll be all right."

The next morning, the doctor called: "When we took out his appendix we found fever blisters all over his insides. He has typhoid." Claire felt a heavy blackness sweep through her body in undulating waves. Charles, listening beside her, turned pale.

"He's sleeping now," the doctor continued. "You can come this afternoon around two o'clock, but only for a little while. He's a very sick little boy."

An hour later, a Public Health Official called at their house. They would all have to be vaccinated, he told them. Three shots each, taken at three-day intervals. He hoped it would not be too late. "We'll need your help in tracking down the source, too," he said. "Typhoid is serious business."

Claire recited the details of their weeks in the country, what they had eaten and where. Charles described the trip home, the places they had stopped. Annette and Nicole and André sat at the other side of the room, staring at the tall thin man: his dark-suited presence had turned them into stones.

That afternoon, Claire and Charles went to see Claude at the hospital. His little body lay strapped to the bed; tubes protruded from his nose and dug into his arms. They were allowed to stay only half an hour; the whole time Claude whimpered, "I want to go home." Claire could hardly bear it.

That evening, after the first set of shots, Nicole's arm swelled to twice its normal size and she ran a low fever. Lying on the sofa, she confronted her dark secret: nobody knew what had made Claude sick. Only she knew. She remembered the soft flesh of his stomach as it yielded to the force of her foot. Now he might die.

"She's having an allergic reaction," the doctor told Claire. "We'll have to discontinue the shots and hope that one will be enough."

Claire sat on the edge of the sofa next to Nicole. The laundry was piling up—clothes she hadn't washed yet from the trip, sheets waiting to be changed. They needed groceries, too; the cupboards were almost bare. Yet she could not bring herself to move. She kept remembering the rented house, the funny odour of the water, the outhouse that had not been limed properly before they came. If she had not insisted on a longer than usual stay, they would not have rented the house. None of this would have happened.

Several days passed and Claude remained in critical condition. The appendectomy had complicated things. Each afternoon, Charles and Claire went to see him for the half-hour they were permitted. Each afternoon, he begged to go home. The LeBlanc house was tense and silent. Nicole burst into tears at odd intervals. Annette and André hung around the backyard, as if they were afraid to leave.

Charles found it harder and harder to concentrate on his business. Sometimes he forgot what the storekeeper had just ordered and carried in the wrong boxes. He kept thinking of Claude, little Claude with his dimples and rosy cheeks and chubby hands—little Claude who might die. He remembered vividly the weeks Claire and the children had been away, how he had missed them. He remembered the joy he had felt when he went to bring them home. And he remembered the flies that had pestered their food in the restaurant on the way back. Those very flies had probably deposited the typhoid on Claude's food. If only he had not insisted on picking them up a week early! A week later, they might have stopped elsewhere, at a place without flies. A dull ache throbbed in his chest all the time now, where these thoughts gathered.

One morning he woke up a little earlier than usual. His chest ached as if an invisible weight had lain on it all night. He had slept badly again, haunted by dreams—Claude's face, pale and gaunt. Flies swarming over him.

58

Claire, sleeping beside him, stirred. A foolish old man, that's what he was, a foolish old man with no patience, overly fond of his young wife. He eased himself out of bed and padded into the kitchen to light the stove. Little pains began shooting down his left arm. He woke Claire.

Now there were two LeBlancs in the hospital. His heart attack was only a mild one, the doctor reassured Claire, but Charles would have to be hospitalized for at least a week. Claude's condition was improving, but he was still not completely out of danger.

It was all Claire could do to keep going. She called as many of Charles' customers as she knew of, told them what had happened, asked them to be patient. She tried not to think about money. Every afternoon she went to the hospital; after she visited Claude, she went to another wing of the hospital to see Charles.

Though she knew Charles had not willed his heart trouble, it began to seem to Claire like a kind of weakness. It was as if he had abandoned them, and during the worst possible time, right in the middle of Claude's crisis. With him gone too, the children became nervous and quarrelsome. André clung to her and sometimes spoke babytalk; Nicole went off by herself and brooded. "Claude and your father are going to be fine," she reassured them. Claude is starting to get better, and so is your father." But they seemed unconvinced. Every night they said the rosary.

The Public Health Official called again. They had tested the well water at the rented house and thoroughly examined the restaurant in Annapolis, he told Claire. There was no trace of typhoid. They had discovered a carrier in Meteghan, however, a woman who lived at the Poor House. Had the LeBlanc family had any contact with her? Claire once again pored over her memory of those weeks in the country—weeks that had seemed so happy and carefree, weeks that now seemed full of danger and treachery.

No, she told him. They had not been anywhere near the Poor House.

After seven days in the hospital, Charles came home. He

needed at least another week of rest, the doctor told Claire. School had just started, and when the children came home he was sitting up in his chair.

"Hi, Dad!" They ran to the chair and hugged him.

"Where's Claude? Didn't he come back with you, Dad?" Nicole looked around the room, expecting to find him.

"He's still sick, so he has to stay a little longer."

"But you came home, how come Claude couldn't? Isn't he ever going to come home?"

"Of course he will, Nicole," Claire said. "He's already a lot better than he was."

"Then how come he can't come home?" Her eyes looked wild.

The source of the typhoid was never discovered. After three and a half weeks in the hospital, Claude was finally allowed to go home. Charles was still weak and unable to work, but he drove to the hospital with Claire and they brought Claude home in the truck. His little body was thin and frail and his eyes had a haunted look. Annette and Nicole and André stared at him, he had changed so. When Claire had to leave him for a moment to go outside for a bucket of coal, he sobbed pitifully, as if he feared she would never return. He needed rest and quiet, the doctor told Claire.

They had fed Claude sparsely in the hospital—something about the typhoid affecting the internal organs—and now that he had permission to eat, he was ravenous. At supper he devoured the food on his plate in a few seconds and begged for more. When Claire made his bed the next morning, she found a wadded up tea biscuit under his pillow.

Later, after the children had left for school, and her two patients were napping, Claire paused for the first time in weeks to look out the front window. Across the street, Mrs. Holland's maple tree blazed with red, and little pools of color were forming underneath. All her life she had faithfully observed the seasons, noting with enthusiasm the small signs that announced the departure of one and the arrival of another. In March, she and the children trooped through the woods in search of the earliest pussywillows; in May, the first Mayflowers. In late August or early September, whenever she spotted the first red leaf she announced it importantly at supper-time. This fall, however, it had all happened without her.

The seasons were rolling on, regardless of the fact that her youngest child had almost died and her husband had had a second heart attack. Bills were piling up on the little telephone table like the leaves under Mrs. Holland's tree. Their savings had dwindled to almost nothing now, and there would be no money except the family allowance check until Charles resumed his rounds. By then they would be deeply into debt.

She thought of the accident five years before and the three grim months that had followed. Back then there had been no family allowance program, so there had been no checks—only trucks from the Red Cross and the Salvation Army. She remembered the humiliation. The crushing sense of helplessness. It could happen again. She was 38 years old. Charles would soon be 63. One of these mornings when she looked across at Mrs Holland's tree she would be a widow with four children to support. Claire felt something hard and bitter form in her chest. Never, never would she allow herself and the children to slip into that terrible poverty again. She would have to prepare herself. But how?

Her own mother had faced the same thing. Her own mother, with five of them to support. With her little store and a hired man to work the land, she had found a way. The Acadians were like that—they survived. She thought of the little church in Grand Pré where the Acadians had been rounded up for the expulsion. She and Isabelle had brought the children there to see it. Against impossible odds, the Acadians had endured as a people. She would find a way, too.

At noon, Annette, Nicole and André came home for dinner. Claude was up and playing with the Lincoln Logs on the living-room floor; Charles was resting in the bedroom. Breathless and rosy from the walk, the children filled the house with their noisy energy. Watching them, Claire felt herself seized by a ferocious love.

Annette threw her coat on the sofa and tousled Claude's hair as she passed. André squatted down beside him and asked what he was making. Nicole, however, hurried through the living-room without looking at him.

It occurred to Claire that Nicole was avoiding Claude. She couldn't remember having seen them together since Claude returned from the hospital. She followed Nicole into the bedroom and watched her lay her coat on the bed.

"Claude is all better," she said gently. "You won't catch anything from him."

"I know!" Nicole flared.

"Then what's wrong? You just ignore him."

Nicole burst into tears.

Claire put her arms around Nicole. "What on earth is the matter?"

"It was my fault," Nicole sobbed. "It was all my fault this happened!"

"It wasn't anyone's fault, silly. It was a germ."

"No no! Don't you see? We had a big fight the day before and I kicked him right in the stomach," she sobbed. "That's what did it!"

Claire thought for a moment. "He already had the typhoid when that happened," she said carefully. "When you kicked him you hurt him inside, but it let us know that something was wrong. That kick may, in fact, have saved his life."

Nicole looked at her uncertainly.

"Do you really think so?"

"Yes."

Nicole's face brightened a little.

Though her words may not have been true, Claire felt that Nicole believed her. And for now, that would have to be enough.

7: School Days

Charles shuffled into the kitchen and lit the stove. It was chilly this morning. The window above the sink was black, but looking out, he could see thin streaks of light in the eastern sky. Frost lay in mysterious folds along the edges of the roofs, the fences, Mrs. Smith's lilac bush. He put the coffeepot on, then cleaned the cats' dishes. He filled one bowl with milk and the other with Kal-Kan, and placed them on the floor.

The cats, gathered at the top of the basement stairs, had heard him and were mewing softly. Clem poked a thick yellow paw through the crack below the door. Quietly, carefully, Charles opened the door and the cats rushed past him into the kitchen. They crowded around the bowls, shouldering each other, growling low threats. After the big ones were full, he would feed the little ones again.

He poured himself some coffee and sat at the table. It was 6.45 AM. By seven, when he called Claire and the children, the kitchen would be warm and cozy. He could relax now, think about things. This sliver of time before the start of a new day seemed almost holy to him. The world was still and safe, Claire and the children peacefully asleep in the neighbouring rooms.

A shrill noise shook the silence. The cats raised their heads, pulled their ears back. Before he could reach the table in the bedroom where the telephone stood, Claire had stretched out her arm and answered it. He heard her voice: "Yes, yes, Gorsebrook School did you say? Yes, I can make it."

She turned on the light and stumbled out of bed.

"That's the third time this week," Charles said.

"I know," Claire replied, "but if I say no they might stop calling me." She pushed past him and headed for the bathroom.

"Could you get some cream of wheat started for the children? I'll have to hurry."

The phone had jolted the children awake, and they began stumbling into the kitchen. They were all arms and legs and jostling bodies. And voices. Talking, quarrelling. Their energy and noise filled the room, filled the whole house.

"I don't want cream of wheat," Claude said. "Yuk!"

"I want toast," André said.

Annette was already at the bread drawer, pulling out the big loaf and a knife to cut it with.

"Cut me one, too," Nicole said. "I want mine with apple sauce. Didn't Mom make apple sauce yesterday?"

Claude stepped on the tail of one of the cats who shrieked

and ran under the stove. "I'm sorry, Solomon," he said, and crawled under the stove to reach him. In the process, he knocked over the milk bowl, and a thin, white stream spread across the floor.

"I need to go number one!" André wailed outside the bathroom door. "Mom! I need to go really bad!"

"I'll be out in a minute," Claire's voice said.

Charles gathered up the cats and put them out the back door. The kitchen was crowded enough without them. As he wiped up the spilled milk, a low anger simmered in him. Before Claire began substitute teaching, he had had no idea it would be this way. She could only accept morning assignments, since Claude was in morning primary, but who would have thought they would call so often? He hadn't liked the idea to begin with, but Claire had insisted. "We *have* to have more money," she had told him simply. "I don't know of any other way."

It was true they needed the money. There was never enough, though he seemed to be working all the time. They were still paying off the hospital bills from over a year ago and the children needed so much. They grew like weeds: their clothes shrank, their toes burst through the sturdiest of shoes. But how he hated these mornings! Each time he saw Claire hurry up the street toward the trolley stop, shame stirred in him.

When Claire came out of the bathroom there was a rush to fill her space. André got in and slammed the door behind him. Annette stood patiently in line, holding her clothes in a little bundle in her arms. For several months now, she had been dressing and undressing in the bathroom. Small nubby breasts protruded through her thick flannel nightgown. Barely twelve, and already she was becoming a woman.

How like Claire she looked, Charles observed, with her dark hair and eyes, that pale skin. Like Claire when she was young. Like Claire before she had begun to harden against him.

Claire was at the vanity now, fixing her hair and face. He watched her line her mouth with lipstick. It amazed him how beautiful she still was.

"Do you want me to take you in the truck?" he asked. "I can take the trolley," she said, "It goes right by. But don't forget to come home right at noon; I won't get home until after the children do. Oh, and tell Annette to... never mind. She doesn't know where they are. Claude's brown pants are dirty. He'll have to wear the green ones."

She got up and rushed into the children's room in her slip and began rummaging in their drawers. "Claude, put these on. And André, wear what you had on yesterday, if your pants are still clean. Did you eat your cream of wheat?"

After they were all gone, Charles finished loading the truck. It took him longer now than it used to. His last heart attack had left his body sluggish, a mass of flesh that didn't always co-operate with his wishes. Before climbing into the truck, he paused for a moment and looked up and down the street. Between 8 and 8:30 AM the little houses had disgorged hundreds of children. They trailed along in bobbing, shifting columns toward the schools—Edgewood, Westmount, St Agnes. Now the houses seemed strangely quiet, abandoned.

Since the city had offered the prefabs for sale, the neighbourhood had changed. People had built stoops and porches, enlarged their kitchens, put in picture windows. And they had painted the little houses in bright colours—yellow or turquoise or pink, or white with brown or green or burgundy trim. The neighbourhood had begun to acquire a settled air, the look of something wild slowly being ordered and tamed. There were fewer rock fights now that sidewalks, curbs and paved roads replaced the gravel roads and dirt paths, and every year a few more picket fences sprang up to protect tiny green yards. Though the children sometimes tore their clothes vaulting them during their mad running games, the fences slowed them down.

Funny what private ownership and prosperity did, he thought. These past few years had been years of record prosperity for Canada—at least that's what all the newspapers said. St. Laurent had even reduced taxes, probably one of the few times in human history a politician had ever reduced regular taxes. Yet what did it mean? Most people were still

65

struggling, and there was still a housing shortage in Halifax. Fancy, expensive houses were springing up in Armdale and along the Northwest Arm, but what good did that do for the average working man like himself?

He examined his own prefab. Two years ago they had painted it white with blue-grey trim, and widened the front steps. Now they simply had to have more room. Four children crammed into one tiny bedroom—it was fine when they were little, but now... He thought of Annette hiding in the bathroom to dress and undress.

The problem was knowing what to do. Some people had transformed the attics of their prefabs into large, dormitory-style rooms with windows at each end. But such rooms were dark, and you could stand up only in the very middle; Claire did not want that. Something had to be done soon, though. The sooner the better.

As Charles began his morning rounds, the fact that he had to be home by noon hung like a weight at the back of his mind. He didn't have time to go all the way to Hollis Street, his usual Thursday morning route, so he called on some customers on Robie and Agricola instead.

"I didn't expect to see you till tomorrow," Lloyd Harris said.

"Well, I was in the neighbourhood, so I thought I'd stop today." Harris was one of his oldest, most loyal customers. He offered Charles a cup of coffee and while he drank it, they talked.

"What do you hear from the dockyards?" he asked. "I'll bet there are a lot of jitters over this new seaway project."

"Oh there are plenty of jitters, all right. I've heard men wonder aloud what will happen to Halifax when ships can go all the way down the Saint Lawrence and into the Great Lakes. They won't have to stop here at all."

Harris always listened carefully to what Charles said about things. Years ago he had followed his column in the *Saint F.X Extension Bulletin*.

"I don't think St. Laurent and his boys worry about the Maritime provinces at all. It's as if we don't exist." He was warming to his subject, now. He could start in on the CCF, protection for the working man against big business. But over Harris' shoulder his eye fell on the wall clock: 11.50 AM.

"Good Lord!" he said. "I have to get going. The wife wants me home at noon, today." He wouldn't tell Harris why. Harris didn't need to know that.

Charles hurried to the truck. Once last week he had forgotten and returned home fifteen minutes late. It was cold out, and the children were huddled by the back door waiting for him, their faces full of reproach.

How he hated hurrying! It made his heart race and his legs ache. Before Claire began substituting, he could look forward to a nice stew or pot of homemade soup on a chilly day like this. But not today. He would rush home to heat up a can of beans or Campbell's soup for everyone, slice a few pieces of bread.

As he rounded the corner of Connaught Avenue and Liverpool Street, Charles saw something that made him stop the truck. There stood a prefab twice the size of any he had seen. A whole second storey had been added, as if the owners had simply raised the roof and added a second layer of rooms below it. So that's how it could be done! There were plenty of windows, he noted, plenty of room for children to spread out in.

By the time he reached the house, his mood was buoyant. He pushed aside the dirty dishes from breakfast and took out the big black skillet. The children needed something warm and filling on a chilly day like today—something like patates et des oeufs. There were boiled potatoes left over from last night's supper and plenty of eggs. He scooped a large dollop of bacon grease from the drippings tin under the sink, and put it in the skillet. As he sliced in some onions, he thought of the address written on a piece of paper in his shirt pocket. Claire would be eager to drive by and look at the house. Maybe they could knock at the door, inquire how it was done. He imagined Claire's face: it had been a long time since she had looked pleased with him.

All morning, Claire had struggled to tame her class of 32 unruly five- and six-year-olds. Now, thank heaven, it was almost over.

67

"Malcolm, you're a big boy, now. You can pick up your own crayons and put them away. And Bonnie, polite little girls don't go around hitting everyone like that."

Oh Lord, there was Clyde, scribbling on Donna's drawing again. What a bunch! Thank heaven she hadn't had this group on her first day of substituting. She might have thrown up her hands and quit. She'd been so nervous that first day. In the past, she had taught mostly in French—only when the subject was English had she spoken it in class—and she had not stood before a class in over eleven years. But her 26 pupils had been sweet and well-behaved, not like this group at all. She'd spent three days with that first class, a nice way of easing herself back in. And it had been silly to worry about the language. Except for a slight accent, she spoke English as well as anyone.

"I don't want to hear any more noise out of yous!" a voice shrilled in the hall. Better than some, she thought to herself.

"It's time to get our coats now," Claire said to the class. "Let's line up quietly and go one by one."

There was a mad rush for the cloakroom, and in the process Clyde fell and cut his knee on the metal leg of the desk. A loud bellow of pain filled the room. "Teacher! Teacher!" voices shrieked. She took him to the nurse's office where they bandaged his kneee. Then she waited with him until his mother came. By the time she boarded the trolley, Claire was exhausted. She thought of her own children, waiting at home for *her*. That was the part she hated the most, not being there when they came home, not having their dinner ready. How would she ever manage if she had to do this full-time? Yet some women with families did. After all these years, School Boards had started hiring them. There were so many children, and few women willing to remain single for the privilege of teaching them.

She leaned into the padded seat of the trolley and tried to relax. She always enjoyed riding the trolley—so many people to observe, to imagine lives for. She scanned the passengers: boyish-looking sailors, high school students carrying armloads of books, housewives wearing kerchiefs over their heads, old people with worn, country faces. Her eyes lingered on a man sitting a few rows ahead. He was around 40, and though she couldn't see his whole face, his dark hair, smooth neck and even profile appealed to her. She studied his smart grey suit and hat and the leather briefcase balanced on his knees. Perhaps he was a banker, or a salesman of some sort. Whatever he did, he had an air of prosperity. She imagined him living in a beautiful, spacious home in the South End, a house with two bathrooms and big trees in the yard. He'd have a pretty wife, too, with a closet full of lovely, expensive clothes; every few years they'd go to Europe.

Suddenly, a wave of envy swept over Claire, envy for this unknown woman with her handsome husband and comfortable life. Except for some twist of fate, it might have been her! Instead, she had to scrimp and save for everything, and rush out of her house in the mornings, leaving everything in chaos. She stared at the man's neck, her heart full of longing.

The man got up and began walking toward her. A little trill of fear seized her. Had he felt her watching him? She formed her face into a pleasant expression in case he might speak. But no, he was headed toward the back exit. As he passed, he moved his eyes over her appreciatively, and she felt herself tingle. She was still attractive; at least she still had that. She became aware, suddenly, of the new jacket and gloves she was wearing, things she had bought with her first paycheque. With her second, she bought two new dresses to wear when she taught. Really, she had a lot to be grateful for. She was lucky they needed teachers so badly, lucky she had gone to Normal School. She thought of Lucille Smith operating a pressing machine in the hot, steamy basement of the Halifax Infirmary.

When she got off the trolley at the corner of Bayers Road, Claire spotted Mrs. Barton coming toward her, holding Ricky and Raymond by the hand. Barbara trailed along a little behind them. The twins attended afternoon primary at Edgewood, and though Barbara was quite capable of bringing them on her way to Westmount, Mrs. Barton always walked them back and forth.

"Why, Mrs. LeBlanc," Mrs. Barton called out. "Are you just getting home? It's just about time for the children to go back to school."

"I know," Claire said wearily. "I was delayed."

"You poor thing," Mrs. Barton said, giving her a sly, superior look. "It's too bad you have to go to work."

"Oh substitute teaching isn't so bad," Claire replied, smiling coldly. "After all, not everyone can do it. It's a good thing I have my education. Education is a wonderful thing."

Mrs. Barton's smug look faltered. Mrs. Barton only had grade 9.

When Claire arrived at the house, the children had finished eating. Their jackets hung haphazardly over the sofa and chairs—why hadn't Charles made them hang them up?—and they were sprawled all over the living-room: Annette and Nicole gawking over the Simpson's Christmas catalogue, André slouching over the remains of a big plate of bread and molasses. The smell of food was like an assault. In her rush that morning, she had eaten only a piece of bread with a cup of Ovaltine. Her head began throbbing, and the residue from her encounter with Mrs. Barton fluttered through her like an unpleasant ether.

What was Charles saying? Something about raising the roof...some house somewhere. He was smiling at her strangely, as if he expected something from her. She found it hard to focus on him. Her eyes kept wandering over his shoulder to the pile of dirty dishes on the counter. It would take her half the afternoon to clean all that up.

8: Raising the Roof

In early May, long before Claire and the children would find the first May flowers, the builders arrived. On one side of the backyard a huge pile of new lumber appeared, smelling fresh and piney, like a walk through Point Pleasant Park. On the other side, a rubble pile sprouted like a fungus, full of old wood, tar paper and broken asbestos shingles.

While he loaded the truck, Charles paused now and then to watch the men. It gave him an odd feeling to see them, scrambling over the top of his house like squirrels. They were all in their thirties and forties, agile and strong. It made his body ache to look at them, bending and stretching, carrying those huge planks of wood.

The whole project, in fact, made him uneasy. He had looked forward to the expansion, knowing how much they needed it, but when the men started taking off the old roof, he was seized with the feeling that things were flying away from him, leaving him suddenly naked, exposed.

One night he found it difficult to sleep knowing that only a thin plaster ceiling separated him from the open area above the house. The feeling was gnawingly familiar. He found himself remembering a ruined bombed-out building in France where they had set up an infirmary during the Great War. He had found it hard to sleep there, too, with the cavernous holes in the walls and roof. The Germans had begun using a new gas—imperceptible at first—against which their gas masks were ineffective. He had seen what this gas could do. On the docks in La Havre where his boat had landed, he had bent over to talk to one of the 600 wounded brought in by a Red Cross train. The man, barely able to breathe, had rasped out an answer. The skin on his throat, around his arm pits and on his upper legs looked as if it had been flayed.

Oh, the war! What had made him think of it, now, some 35 years later! It was this roofless house.

Other starry nights from the war came back to him now. Nights on the SS Urania, on the way over. Though the war was new to them then, they had heard of the German submarines and their diabolical efficiency. The Urania was an old ship, and he and the other enlisted men, crammed deep in the ship's belly, openly wondered how they would fare if she were torpedoed or caught fire. When they entered the war zone, many of them brought up their blankets and slept on the open deck. At least the lifeboats were nearby, supplied with biscuits and water.

No, he would not let himself think of the war. The war they had believed would end all wars! He turned toward Claire sleeping beside him, her face half buried in the pillow. She stirred and rolled over, away from him. In a few days the space above the house would be completly enclosed: he would sleep better then.

When they were not in school, the LeBlanc children combed the rubble pile in the backyard. It was here that Charles found Nicole and André, lifting up loose boards and throwing them from one side of the pile to the other. Minou and Clem crouched by the pile, watching for terrified, fleeing fieldmice.

"How many times do I have to tell you to stay out of that old woodpile!" he bellowed through the back door.

"We need this stuff for our camp," Nicole protested. They had been working on a half-built shack for weeks.

"I've told you over and over! That wood is full of rusty nails. Get one in your foot and and you could get lockjaw. Now get out of there right now and stay out!" He had seen a man die of lockjaw once, during the war.

Nicole tiptoed off the pile. She couldn't imagine how getting a nail in your foot could have anything to do with your jaw. Besides, each of them had stepped on a nail at least once so far and other than having to soak their feet in hot salted water, nothing had happened. "We'll just have to wait till he goes down to the basement," she whispered to André.

Charles watched them for a few moments to make sure they did as they were told. He could feel the redness in his face, the pulsing in his temples. Those children made him so angry! The minute he was out of sight they would probably go right back to the rubble pile.

A wave of tiredness swept over him. What was the use! He shuffled into the living-room and sank into his chair. It was only four o'clock and he still had a few more calls to make—he had come home to pick up some more potato chips—but he could rest his legs for a moment. Claire would not be back for another half-hour. She had taken Claude and gone to see the school board about substituting again next year. How glad he would be when school ended for the summer and Claire stayed home, the way it used to be!

Everything was changing, it seemed. Claire gone almost every day, the house torn apart, the children finding new and more complex forms of mischief. Perhaps it was this constant flux, this never knowing what was going to happen each day, this chaos, that had made him remember the war.

He hoisted himself out of his chair and slowly descended the basement stairs. Maybe Claire would make something good for supper.

By the end of June, the outer frame was complete. A new wooden staircase just inside the front door joined the old house to its new addition. From the outside, the upstairs looked finished: two large windows faced east, two faced west, and a smaller one faced south; new asbestos shingles covered the area in between. The inside, however, consisted of only one huge, unfinished room. Rough flooring had been put down, but the walls were open to the outer frame, and the shiny tips of nails attaching the shingles from the outside poked through.

The contractor wanted what seemed to be a huge amount of money just to finish off two of the three planned rooms, so construction came to a halt.

"Couldn't we sleep up there anyway?" Annette wanted to know. "We could move our bed up and everything," Nicole added. "It would be like sleeping outside."

"It's full of sawdust," Claire replied.

"And there's no electricity yet," Charles added.

"What will we do, then?" Annette asked.

Claire looked at Charles and her mouth tightened. "A lot of men are handy," she said. "They know how to do things."

"Oh don't worry, we'll get it done one way or another," Charles said. They were having rice soup for supper. It wasn't one of his favourite meals, but Claire had made a gingerbread for dessert. He eyed it on the counter.

"Maybe we could find a carpenter," Claire suggested. "A family man who works and takes other jobs in his spare time. A man like that would probably charge less and be glad of the extra money."

They found Mr. McNair through a school teacher in Dartmouth Claire had met while substituting. He was a cheerful presence with a shiny, rosy face and a large mouth full of white teeth. During the day he worked at the dockyards; from 5.30 to 9.30 PM, he hammered and sawed and whistled upstairs at the LeBlanc house. On Saturdays, he arrived at 9.00

73

AM and stayed until 9.00 PM, sometimes going home for an hour around suppertime. Sundays he spent with his family.

Nicole liked to watch Mr. McNair work. Muscles rippled along his arms and neck when he lifted things, and he smelled nice, the way her uncles in Digby smelled when they worked in the barn or baled hay. His tool chest was interesting, too, full of little compartments, like a giant jewellery box. He knew how to put wires together so there would be a light in the ceiling and a place to plug in things. And he guessed who the two new rooms were for: one for her parents; and one for her and Annette.

Every evening and twice on Saturday, her mother went upstairs to check Mr. McNair's progess. Before she did, she paused at the vanity to powder her nose and put on fresh lipstick. "Do you want to come up?" she asked Nicole.

"Sure," Nicole said.

When he saw her mother, Mr. McNair looked up from the piece of wood he was planing and smiled.

"My, things are really coming along!" her mother said. Whenever she talked to Mr. McNair, her mother seemed suddenly light, as if she were standing on her toes.

"Well, we're making progress, anyway." Mr. McNair's face turned pink, and the two big dimples on his cheeks bent in.

"I brought you a little dish of peaches," her mother said, holding out a glass bowl with a spoon. "You can't have had much of a dinner." She looked over at Mr. McNair's black lunchbucket. Nicole looked too.

"Oh, I can't complain," Mr. McNair said, "but thank you very much." He took the dish and began eating the peaches. His whole face and neck glowed red.

On Saturday afternoons her mother always brought him something. Sometimes it was only a glass of Kool-aid; other-times it was a piece of pie left from dinner. And always, his face and neck turned red. When Nicole's father turned red it meant he was angry; when Mr. McNair turned red it looked like his whole body was smiling.

"And how are the twins?" Her mother asked. Mr. McNair had twin daughters who were three years old, and every few days her mother asked about them. Her voice, when she talked to Mr. McNair, had a lovely purring sound, which Nicole tried to imitate standing in front of the bathroom mirror.

"Oh, they're just fine. Getting into everything all the time, but just as cute as can be. Here, let me show you something." He put down the empty bowl and took a picture out of his wallet.

Her mother said: "How pretty they are! Look, Nicole, aren't they pretty?"

Mr McNair smiled with his big white teeth. It surprised Nicole that her mother would be so interested in Mr. McNair's daughters. They really weren't very pretty at all. They were the only children besides her own that her mother had ever been so interested in.

"Well, I'd better let you get back to work," her mother said. Her voice had little trills in it now, as if she were singing.

When her mother left, Mr McNair's face went back to its normal colour. Nicole watched him hammer for a while, then went downstairs. Her mother's voice had returned to normal, too.

At supper her mother said: "What a good worker Mr. McNair is! He's determined to get ahead. He wants to take good care of his family."

Nicole looked at her father to see if he agreed. But he kept his head bent and ate silently.

When Mr. McNair was not there, Nicole and Annette and André and Claude were allowed to play upstairs as long as they promised to be careful and not disturb Mr. McNair's things. It was a perfect place for play. Long low eaves stretched along the front and back of the house, large enough for a child to crawl through. Gaps in the plywood flooring formed useful nooks for hiding secret messages.

One day, while Nicole was playing upstairs with her new friend Joanne she heard a series of tiny, high-pitched noises coming from an area under the floor.

"Did you hear that?"

Joanne put her ear near the floor. "It sounds like little babies crying, far, far away." Joanne had nine little brothers and sisters.

"Oh my gosh!" Nicole exclaimed. "It must be Minou! She's

supposed to be having babies any day now. She can't have them down there under the floor. They might go crawling all over the place and never find the openings. And what if Mr. McNair boards up the holes? We've got to get her out!"

They wedged their faces into the gaps and called and coaxed and encouraged. But Minou refused to appear.

When Charles came home for supper several hours later, he was met by Nicole, her face flushed and her blue eyes blazing.

"You've got to help, Dad!"

By then, Annette, André, Claude and even Claire had all tried calling and whistling for Minou, but none had been successful. The children were excited and nervous, and when Charles began to mount the stairs with his slow, heavy steps, they urged him to hurry.

"You're all making such a big racket," he told them. "No wonder Minou's afraid."

Kneeling on the floor by the opening to the eave, he bent his big body toward the holes in the floorboards. Because of the joists, Minou would have to come out the same way she got in. The children kept very still; he could feel them holding their breath. He whispered and cooed and called Minou's name coaxingly. Minou almost always came when he called. Sure enough, in a little while she emerged, looking thin and bedraggled, but purring, and carrying a damp lump of fur in her mouth. He took it from her gently and examined it.

"It's dead," he said. The children moaned.

"What about the others?" Nicole asked. "There must be others."

There was a loose piece of plywood, not completely nailed down, where Minou had emerged. Charles pried it off and found half of a small furry body. The other half had been chewed off. The children gasped.

"What could have done that?" Annette asked. Her face was twisted in disgust and horror. "Could it be rats?"

"Rats! You mean we have rats?" André asked.

Charles felt a shiver of fear pass through the children. "No," he said. He hated to tell them, but he couldn't have them thinking it was rats. "Minou probably killed the kittens herself and ate some of them," he said.

A roar of protest rose from the children. "Not Minou! She wouldn't do a thing like that!"

"Mother cats sometimes kill their babies if they think they're in danger," he explained. "She probably panicked. She's so young, she's just a kitten herself really. She didn't know what to do." He held her in his arms and stroked her gently. "The poor thing. She shouldn't have been having babies so young anyway. That darn Clem!"

Nicole stared at Minou, who was trembling and purring at the same time. Mothers were supposed to protect their babies, fiercely if necessary, not kill them and eat them.

Later that evening, Nicole went over to Joanne's to tell her what had happened. Joanne lived two blocks away in a four-room pre-fab similar to Nicole's. Joanne's father had built a large addition onto the kitchen and a long screened-in porch. Nicole walked through the porch to the kitchen door, carefully stepping over the mattresses laid out on the floor. Once, when she came by for Joanne early one Saturday morning, she had stumbled over the sleeping bodies of four of Joanne's brothers, sprawled on the mattresses in rumpled street clothes.

In response to Nicole's knock, Joanne opened the door a crack and said: "I'll be right out. Meet me around front." Nicole had never been inside Joanne's house and often wondered what it was like. She wondered, especially, where they all slept when it was too cold for the boys to sleep on the porch. In the front, Nicole found Joanne's mother sitting on the steps, holding the littlest baby. Two of the smallest children were climbing over her.

Mrs. MacDonald always looked the same. Her dark brown hair hung in a tangle around her ears and she always seemed to be wearing the same dress. She never wore powder and lipstick like Nicole's mother did, but her eyes were bright and sharp. She liked to throw her head back and laugh, showing rounded pink gums where her teeth had once been. Every year she had a new baby.

When Joanne appeared, Mrs. MacDonald said: "Don't forget, you have to go to the store."

On the way, Nicole told Joanne about Minou eating her babies. Joanne made horrified, disgusted noises.

At Dan's, Joanne bought a big bag of small, firm oranges, and Nicole suggested that they eat one.

Joanne eyes opened in alarm. "My mother would kill me!"

"What for?" Nicole was astounded.

"We're not allowed to eat them. They're for my mother and father."

"But that's not fair!" Nicole sputtered. "At our house we eat everything."

"My mother says they're too expensive for us kids," Joanne said. "She has to eat them because the doctor told her to, and my father gets to because he works so hard."

"Well I think that's really selfish of them. Imagine them not letting you kids have any!"

Joanne looked at the ground and said nothing. She was thin and quiet and never argued with Nicole. That was one of the reasons Nicole liked her.

On her way home, Nicole thought again of Mrs. MacDonald and the oranges. Maybe Mrs. McDonald had been too young when she started having babies.

By the time school started in September, the two upstairs rooms were almost finished. In the evenings when she tried to do her homework, Nicole found it hard to concentrate. How could she, with the sound of Mr. McNair's rollers and brushes slap-slapping against the walls upstairs, and that lovely painty smell drifting down. Each evening she went up to look. Mr. McNair had stained the wood around the large window a yellow-brown, like nuts. Through the window, over the tops of the trees, she could see a pale purple sky. This is where I will stand each morning when I get up, she thought. This is what I will see when I sit at the desk.

Mr McNair had painted the closet, too, where she and Annette would hang their clothes. Her blue dress. Annette's yellow one. Their shoes would rest on the floor below like little peaceful feet, like peas lined up in a square pod. There would be no boys with their sour-smelling socks and balled-up dirty underwear. They would keep their things in those cubbies under the eaves—her paint sets, Annette's rock and leaf collections, their games. There would be no trucks or

Lincoln logs or pieces of erector set to hurt their bare feet. All that space. For just her and Annette.

One day, a truck brought two rolls of new linoleum, one for each new bedroom. Two burly men carried them upstairs, their big, booted feet thunking on the steps. Mr. McNair, grinning and whistling, cut them and tacked them down. A few days later the Simpson's truck brought a new chest of drawers and a small desk for Nicole and Annette to share. With the white wrought iron bed brought up from downstairs, their room was complete. Annette set up her microscope set on the desk and put in a little glass plate. "Isn't this great?" she beamed. When Nicole went to put her games in the cubby under the eaves, she found Minou, sniffing around as if she had lost something.

A few days later, the Simpson's truck came again, bringing a bed, chest of drawers and a matching desk for the other room. But that night, only her mother came upstairs to go to bed.

"Isn't Dad coming up too?" Nicole asked.

"Your father snores and keeps me awake," her mother said. "I have to have a good night's sleep if I'm to teach."

Her mother was folding back the corner of the bedclothes, not looking at her. She looked different, somehow, like someone Nicole didn't know.

When she went downstairs to go to the bathroom, Nicole looked into her parents' old room. Her father was sitting up in bed, reading.

"It's nice up there," she said, because she couldn't think of anything else to say.

"Those stairs are too hard for me to climb all the time," he answered.

9: Small Fry

"Just stay in the truck while I go in the store," Charles said. "They'll see you and stay away."

Nicole hunched in the passenger seat, her door locked, the windows rolled up tightly. The *they* who would see her and stay away were thieves, usually boys, who crept to the truck after it got dark, pried open a door or one of the windows, grabbed a few boxes of candy, and ran—all while her father was inside taking an order. This was Nicole's first time on Gottingen Street, and darkness had begun falling like rain.

The buildings around her seemed to blend in a dark blur of brown and grey or dark green or faded barn red, unlike the bright white and pink and turquoise houses of her own neighbourhood. Narrow, and two or three storeys high, they crowded together as if for protection. Some of them leaned forward a little, or to one side, as if a fierce blow had sent them reeling. Front doors opened onto sidewalks. Even the streetlights seemed dim.

A pair of boys lurched out from a small space between two buildings. Their eyes flashed toward Nicole and a tremor of fear ran up and down her legs. What if they tried to pry open one of the truck windows right in front of her? How would she stop them? But the boys, bare armed in the cool September evening, went into the store where her father was.

A woman with long stringy hair and bright pink lipstick stood against the lamppost and lit a cigarette. Nicole studied the way she threw her head back when she exhaled, the way her eyes darted from side to side as if she knew someone was watching her, the way she pulled her frayed wool jacket up to her neck, then let it slide down over her shoulders.

An old man with a raggedy, dirty coat stumbled by, carrying a paper bag with a bottle sticking out. He paused between two buildings, his back to the road, his legs apart, looking over his shoulders every few seconds, the way her father did when he peed in the basement drain, careful to avoid her mother's eye. Finished, the old man pulled himself up and slunk over toward the woman and said something to her. She barked something back and spat at him. Nicole rolled down her window as fast as she could, hungry for words. Too late. The old man ducked between two buildings, and the woman walked down the street, flinging her head back.

The air smelled of salt and fish. The waterfront, vast and mysterious, lay only a few blocks away.

In a few moments her father came out. "Is everything okay?"

80

"Fine."

He went around to the back of the truck, unfastened the chain and padlock, and reached for a box of coconut balls and two boxes of jawbreakers. The back doors had been pried open so many times the regular lock no longer worked.

"Come sit in the back while I take these in. Otherwise half the truck will be gone by the time I come back."

Nicole scampered over the boxes and sat between the open doors. The darkness had thickened now, and she imagined eyes, dozens of them, staring at her from the dark buildings, from the dark cracks between them. But no thieves came. She thumped her legs against the bumper, feeling, suddenly, very powerful.

Her father came back for two cartons of potato chips, then closed and locked the back doors. "I'll only be a few minutes more," he said.

A sudden riot of sound drew Nicole's attention to a group of sailors on the other side of the street. They were laughing and singing and patting each other's backs and shoulders. Navy-blue trousers hugged their hips; their white hats, cocked over their foreheads, caught and held the light. She had never seen sailors so close before, and strained to see the details of their faces.

A short, stout woman all dressed in black hurried by the truck with her little girl. The girl, who had the same yellow-brown skin and black hair as her mother, said something in a language Nicole could not identify. It was not English, but neither was it the French they used to speak at home. Sharp, guttural sounds drifted toward her open window.

When her father finally appeared he said, "Now that wasn't so hard, was it?" From her window Nicole stared into the night, thrilling to the strangeness of the place, so unlike anything she had ever known.

Charles was recovering from a mild heart attack, his third. Back at his rounds, he hauled his big body around, creaking and aching. This Friday evening he was almost too tired to take off his jacket, to unlace his boots, to put on the worn, soft slippers, to lower himself into the embracing curves of the chair. He lifted his legs, one at a time, onto the hassock.

Nicole, her mother and the boys were curled on the big davenport with a blanket and two of the cats. An eerie, blue-grey light flickered through the room. They were watching Perry Mason.

"I don't know how I'm going to make it," her father said. "Tomorrow is my busiest day." His breathing was heavy and laboured, like air tubes full of gravel. Her mother blamed his weight for his chronic tiredness, his heart trouble, his high blood pressure. They had all heard her tell him, usually at mealtime, that he ate too much.

"Why don't you take one of the children to help," she suggested, shifting her position to look at him. A wave of adjustment swept through the pile of tangled arms and legs. Clem jumped to the floor where he yawned and arched his back.

"They can do more than just guard the truck now and then, you know. They could help carry things."

"I suppose so," her father said. "Lord knows I could use some help." He leaned around and looked at them: "Which one of you wants to go with me to Spryfield?" Della Street was about to say something important to Perry so no-one said anything. The furnace grunted on and the whole house trembled.

"Put on your old clothes," her mother told her. "So you don't ruin your good ones." When Nicole objected, her mother said: "The others will have to take their turns, too."

By 9.30 AM the truck was loaded, and they were ready to go. They passed the North West Arm, where the thumb of water looked cold and menacing, and on up the hill to Spryfield. The air felt damp and grey and Nicole thought with some resentment of the Monopoly game she had planned to play with Joanne. The road was bumpy; she curled her fingers under the seat and held on. The truck groaned and lurched. The boxes in the back shifted and creaked.

They stopped at a small square building flanked by ragged clumps of black spruce. Billows of dust flew up as they pulled into the unpaved drive. Two boys, squatting on the ground by the front door, leaped up when they saw the truck. "It's the Candyman!" one of them yelled. "The Candyman's here!"

"Well, the Candyman at last." The storekeeper held out his hand to her father. "And how are you feeling, Charles?"

"A lot better but still not so good." Her father leaned on the counter and took off his cap. The skin on his forehead looked thin and pink. "They kept me in the hospital for five days," he said.

Nicole was not sure what to do while they talked. The two boys were staring at her, so she studied the meat case with its fat tubes of baloney and sausage, the reddish brown slabs.

"I have to be careful," her father continued. "At 66 a man isn't what he used to be."

A big yellow cat slept coiled by the oil stove in the corner of the store. Nicole went over to pat him. "Nice puss, puss." The cat rolled over and offered his big belly.

"Nicole, bring in two cartons of potato chips for Mr. Comeau," her father said. "We'll also need a box of spearmint leaves, one of jawbreakers and one of liquorice babies." The boys watched her go in and out, their eyes big, their mouths wordless.

The next store was busy with shoppers. A little girl and her mother stood at the glass case by the pennycandy. "Ah, the Candyman's here," the storekeeper said. The girl and her mother turned to look at Nicole's father, made way for him.

At noon they stopped for fish and chips at a tiny place with a small counter and a few stools. Shelves full of Campbell's soup and canned meat and spaghetti lined the walls. A woman brought them fish and chips from somewhere in the back. Nicole carefully unfolded the newspaper wrapping and gobbled down the hot breaded fish and the soft, salty strips of potato. At home, they were probably having canned soup.

By mid-afternoon they were all the way to Herring Cove. The store there was large and new. Next to the soda fountain stood the largest display of comicbooks Nicole had ever seen. While her father told the store keeper about his heart attack, she leafed through the Little Lulu comics. A girl about her age looked up from an Archie comic and asked, "Is that your grandpa?" "No," Nicole said. "It's my father." The girl blinked and adjusted her glasses. Her eyes looked enormous behind them.

"You've got a good helper, I see," the storekeeper said as Nicole carried in the order. She pretended not to hear him.

"Oh she's a good helper all right," her father said.

"And pretty, too," the storekeeper added. "Just wait till some boy comes along and steals her away from you." "This one's too smart for that," her father said. Nicole tried not to smile but she could feel the corners of her mouth edging upward.

"I think your helper could use some ice cream." The storekeeper said, pulling out a wafer cone. "How about strawberry?" He waved a big, shiny scoop.

On the way home, Nicole asked her father: "Can I come with you next Saturday, too? "

A small man with round wire-rimmed glasses and a briefcase came to the front door. Unsmiling in his dark grey suit and vest, he looked as if he would cringe if someone touched him. Her father hurried him through the living-room and down to the basement. Her mother followed the man with sharp, cold eyes but said nothing. In the basement her father and the man talked in hushed voices and rustled papers. They were still down there when everyone else went to bed.

"How come you don't sell chocolate bars or ten-cent bags of candy like humbugs and chicken bones?" Nicole asked. They were loading the truck for Spryfield.

"Those big companies only sell to the big wholesalers."

"All the kids at school buy Cadbury bars and Coffee Crisps and Cherry Blossoms. I bet we could sell a lot of them."

"Well there's no use thinking about it because it won't happen," her father growled. "Those big companies don't want to bother with small fry like me."

"What do you mean?"

"I can only buy a few cartons at a time. They'd have to send their big trucks here to deliver them and they don't think it's worth it."

"But that's not fair! Why don't you just keep pestering them, until they say yes?"

"It's not that simple, Nicole."

The small man with round wire-rimmed glasses and the briefcase came again. There was more talk, more paper shuffling in the basement at her father's big desk.

"Some accountant!" her mother hissed after the man left. "He's a crook! You're paying taxes on money you never earned and you pay him a huge fee for that."

"That's pure foolishness, Claire," her father said, "and you know it."

"Well where is all the money he says you earn?" she countered. "Can you tell me that?"

Nicole sat on the basement stairs thinking about her father. It's not that simple, he'd said. And yet it seemed to her that the whole thing *was* simple: you bought things, you sold them for more than you paid, and you kept the difference. It was just like the greeting cards she sold from door to door after school. She thought of her little blue notebook with its rows of figures, the line that said profit: $6.34.

The basement had become a murky place, cluttered and stinky. Though the area around the candy shelves was relatively neat, the rest was littered with junk: Claude's old tricycle missing one of its wheels, half-filled cans of hardened paint, old truck tires, snow chains, a bureau with its drawers broken and yawning. A huge circle of dark oil stained the cement floor where her father pulled in the truck at night.

Small fry, he'd called himself.

Nicole looked at the drainage ditch where her father still peed, though he told her mother he didn't do that anymore. "It's too hard for me to go up and down the stairs all the time," he muttered when Nicole caught him at it. Along the wide basement doors lay shrivelled strips of cucumber peel, put there to keep out the ants; now they were slowly rotting.

Under a window near the candy shelves sat her father's huge wooden desk, its top littered with carbon copies of letters, broken pencils, paper clips, wadded up piles of paper. Nicole thought of her father and the man sitting at the desk, the hushed talk, her mother's anxious face.

All of a sudden she was furious at the mess, the disorder, the unfairness of things. In a rush of energy, she swept the cement floor, threw out the cucumber peels, tidied the junk, covered the oil stains with scraps of old linoleum, and flushed out the drainage ditch with two buckets of hot soapy water. Her father's desk came next. She threw out the wadded paper and broken pencils and sorted the letters into neat piles, putting all the orders in one, and bills in another. Finally, she dusted everything with a soft rag soaked in lemon oil.

When she was all finished, she sat in her father's chair. Everything looked and smelled a lot better. Then it occured to her: she could get him a little book. A sudden picture formed: the little book, neat columns of figures, a girl who looked like her writing things down. He's not a small fry, she would tell the big candy companies. See?

10: Blue Coat

"It was the bluest blue," Nicole told her mother. "Like the sky in summer, when the clouds get fat and white." Her mother handed her two bowls of clam chowder to put on the table. Annette cut several slabs of bread from the big double loaves and put them on a pink melmac plate.

"You should have seen the way it looked with my eyes. When I tried it on, my eyes looked bluer than blue." "Put the molasses on the table, too," her mother said. "For André." André practically lived on fried baloney and bread and molasses. Since this was Friday, there'd be no baloney.

When they were all sitting down, Nicole tried again. "It was so gorgeous," she said in her best dreamy, sing-song voice. "It was the new balloon style, you should have seen it."

"What's all this?" her father asked.

"She's got her eye on a spring coat," her mother said. Nicole looked at her father hopefully, but all he said was, "Pass the bread and butter."

"I haven't had a new coat in ages," she persisted. "Annette got a new one last year."

Annette made a shrieking sound, as if she'd been accused of something shameful. "My old one didn't fit me anymore!"

"Hurry up and eat your supper," her father said. "We've got a big night ahead." Nicole hadn't started her chowder yet. All she could think of was the blue coat.

"Honestly, that girl never eats. She lives on hopes and cold water."

"Some other people don't know when to stop eating," her mother said, eying her father's big stomach. Her father's face stiffened; the folds on his neck shook like a turkey wattle.

"Don't start that again," he said.

No-one said anything and the kitchen filled with slurping sounds. Claude chewed with his mouth open and her mother didn't tell him to close it. Not a good time to tell her how much the coat cost, Nicole decided.

Later, while she helped her father load the truck, Nicole thought again about the coat. Even the old wool jacket she had on wasn't new when she got it. Her mother had bought it from an ad in the *Chronicle-Herald*, making her promise never to tell. The sleeves were two inches too short now, so Nicole wore it with her other old clothes when she helped her father. For school she had a better coat that used to be Annette's.

Annette seemed to get everything these days, Nicole thought bitterly. Annette and her big pointy breasts. Mr. McNair had been back hammering and sawing upstairs and had made the space across the hall into a room for Annette. Now all she did was close the door and play records and whisper things with her friend Babbette.

"I'll need six more boxes of chocolate bunnies," her father called out, wheezing. He was rearranging cartons inside the truck, putting the candy they sold most of near the back doors.

Nicole knew exactly where everything was. Every few weeks she straightened out all the candy shelves. When things were out of place her father sometimes got confused and ordered things he didn't need. When new shipments came, she unpacked the cartons and put the new boxes in the back to make sure they sold the old ones first. She handed her father the bunnies. "How about jelly beans? We sold a lot of them last weekend."

"I have some here, but a few more boxes wouldn't hurt." His voice sounded like bones creaking. His face was dark red.

As they started out down the street, her father said, "I don't know what I'd do without you, Nicole." For over a year now she'd been going in the truck with him on Friday nights and all day Saturday. She knew that was not all he meant, though. When her mother and father quarrelled—all the time now, it seemed—they tried to get the kids on their side. Sometimes she was on her father's side, sometimes her mother's. Right now she didn't care. All she could think of was the beautiful blue coat she would probably never own.

Their first stop was McDougal's Grocery on the corner of Oxford and Young. "I see you've got your good little helper with you," Mr. McDougal said. He had curly red hair mixed with grey and he liked to tease.

"Go get Mr. McDougal two boxes of duck eggs, one of blackballs and two cartons of potato chips," her father said.

When she carried in all the boxes at once, Mr. McDougal grinned and said, "She's just as good as a boy."

"She's better," her father said. "I'd much rather have her along than *both* her brothers." After a while Nicole forgot about the blue coat.

On Monday morning at recess, Nicole asked Joanne: "Are you getting anything new for Easter?" "A new skirt and blouse," Joanne said. There were twelve kids in Joanne's family now, and at Easter, Christmas and just before school started in the fall, her mother ordered them all something from the Simpson's catalogue. "Are you?"

"I don't know," Nicole said. "Probably." It wouldn't be the blue coat, she thought gloomily. She fished some candy eggs from her pocket and handed two to Joanne. One of the boxes had broken open during the Saturday rounds.

"I really shouldn't eat these," Joanne said. "I gave up candy for Lent." She put the yellow one in her mouth and chewed it solemnly.

In a corner of the schoolyard, Diane and Gloria, the two

most popular girls, stood in a circle of friends. Duncan McKenzie and Ronnie Solari watched them from a few feet away. Next to Duncan's pink face, Ronnie's olive skin looked even more yellow-brown than usual. Nicole thought of the dream she'd had a few weeks before. She was pulling the clothes basket out from under her father's bed and found Ronnie, curled up in the basket. He leaped out and started chasing her. Soon they were outside, running near the bushes at the end of her street. Then Ronnie caught her, and they tumbled around on the ground punching and pinching each other. Nicole had him pinned when suddenly his skin stuck to her hands. She tried to get it off, but it just stretched out. Ronnie lay still then, staring at her with his black eyes, his skin stretching from her hands, all yellowy brown and shiny like molasses toffee.

When she woke up she was sweating and feeling like she might throw up. She hadn't been able to look at Ronnie since then without feeling queasy.

"Do you want this last egg?" she asked Joanne. "I'm not hungry anymore."

"What if I helped pay for it with my allowance?" Nicole asked. Her mother had just gotten back from the school in Dartmouth where she taught. The grade three teacher there had gotten TB, so her mother taught full-time now. It took her over an hour to get home; she took the trolley and had to transfer twice.

"Fifty cents a week will hardly make a difference in a coat that costs $24.95," her mother said. Nicole watched her change from her good dress into an old housedress.

"I have $8.75 saved up, you could have that, too." She was getting fairly close to throwing herself at her mother's feet and begging.

Her mother turned and looked at her strangely. Her lipstick had worn off and her nose was shiny. "You really want that coat a lot, don't you?"

Easter morning was sunny and glorious. Four Easter baskets made of wide strips of purple, yellow, pink and green straw shone like spring bouquets on the dropleaf table. Nicole's father had bought them from a Micmac Indian who sold them door-to-door, saying he felt sorry for him. Now each held a flat round of maple sugar, an assortment of pennycandy from the basement, and a large foil-wrapped chocolate bunny bought from a store.

"Stay away from those baskets," André warned Claude. Claude had already eaten one of the ears off his bunny, and since he had broken the fast and couldn't go to Holy Communion now, he was sneaking more bites whenever he could. He grinned at André like a cat, his face white as milk, his hair glossy black. "Claude should have to wait like the rest of us!" André yelled.

They were getting ready for Mass. Annette and her mother sat at the vanity in her father's room, dabbing lipstick on their mouths. Her mother didn't say anything. Claude was her pet. None of this bothered Nicole. She was too busy looking over their shoulders at the girl in the mirror: a girl with a blue coat and the bluest eyes. She could hardly believe that girl was her.

"Nicole must be cold," Annette said to no-one in particular. "She's had that coat on for the last half-hour."

"You look nice," her father said from the doorway, blinking, as if he were half-surprised.

It took them a long time to get to the church. Though it was only two-and-a-half blocks away, it was uphill and her father walked slowly. Nicole held his arm, and for once, her mother didn't tell him to hurry up. The sun warmed their faces; her mother admired the yellow and purple crocuses struggling up in a few front yards. By the time they arrived, all the back seats were taken, so they had to sit near the front.

Overnight, the church had been transformed. The purple sacks that had covered the statues all during Lent had disappeared, and huge pots of white Easter lillies gleamed from the altar. Rosy-gold light spilled through the stained-glass windows onto the pews, making everything look fresh and cheerful. The church was teeming with people, and it seemed as if everyone was wearing something bright or new for Easter.

Nicole spotted Diane sitting a few rows back on the other side. She was wearing a pretty new spring coat, cream-coloured, with a large collar, but not the new balloon style. As far as Nicole could tell, no-one had a coat quite like hers. She glanced around again, just to be sure, and saw Ronnie Solari looking right at her. Other people noticed her, too. When she went to communion she felt their eyes. She held her head up and looked straight ahead. She had never felt like this before, never in her whole life. Was this what it was like to be pretty?

There was no school on Easter Monday, but on Tuesday Nicole wore her new blue coat. At the corner someone came up behind her. It was Ronnie. "Hi," he said with a smile. The black curls on his forehead jiggled. She watched his yellow neck as he crossed the street, too stunned to move. This was the first time Ronnie had ever spoken to her.

Later, at recess, Joanne began telling her what her three-year-old sister had done with the hard-boiled eggs on Easter morning, but Nicole had a hard time paying attention. Her eyes kept wandering over the schoolyard, past the little girls playing jump rope, over to the hoop where the boys were taking turns throwing a basketball. Ronnie was among them.

"What's the matter with you!" Joanne jerked Nicole's arm. "You're not even listening."

"I am," Nicole said, and made herself look right at Joanne.

"Well anyway," Joanne continued, "we finally found the eggs under the bed, all squashed, so we had to have puffed wheat for breakfast instead."

"Hmm." Nicole nodded her head.

"Well, don't you think that's funny?"

"I heard that Ronnie Solari smokes," Nicole said. Her eyes had wandered over to the hoops again.

"Who cares!" Joanne said. "He's a creep anyway."

Nicole studied Ronnie's face, the shadow of dark hair above his thin mouth. "You're right," she said. "He is."

When she got home André was making himself a plate of bread and molasses. The sight of it made her stomach tighten.

The following Friday, Nicole and her father loaded up the rest of the Easter goods. "I'll have to sell it half price in order to get rid of it," he said.

"We'll eat it if you don't," she grinned.

"That's just the trouble. You kids already eat more candy than I sell." He pulled a yellow pencil from under an arm of his wire-rimmed glasses and began checking things off on a list.

It had turned cold again, so Nicole pulled the woollen toque she had borrowed from André down over her ears. As she leaned over the back of the truck, the left knee of her dungarees caught on a rusted edge and tore.

"There probably won't be much business tonight," her father grumbled. "It's been bad all week."

"Oh, don't worry, Dad," she said, giving him a hug.

Their first stop, as usual, was McDougal's on Oxford Street. As Nicole carried in the order, she felt someone watching. Perhaps it was a thief getting ready to grab something from the truck the minute she went inside. She looked around and for a split second her eyes met someone else's. *Ronnie!* He turned and pretended he hadn't seen her. All at once Nicole was aware of how she was dressed. Her face got red hot, and she almost dropped the boxes. Ronnie disappeared around the corner.

"It's a good thing you've got that good helper," Mr. McDougal said when she came in. One of his green eyes winked.

For the rest of the evening, Nicole felt strange. Twice she got the orders mixed up and had to go back to the truck for something she forgot. A funny sick feeling hovered at the bottom of her stomach. Her old wool jacket felt heavy, like a dull, flat weight. She picked at the threads around the hole at her knee.

By the time they finished the evening rounds it was nearly nine o'clock. Her father pulled the truck into the basement and closed the big wooden doors from inside. Nicole handed him the iron bar he propped against the doors to keep out thieves. She needed to tell him something but she was not sure how.

"Dad," she said. "I don't think I want to go in the truck with you anymore."

Her father looked at her. "I thought you liked going." His big hands hung by his side.

"I did," she said staring at her old sneakers. "But I don't want to go anymore. You can get one of the boys to help."

Her father didn't reply right away. His breathing sounded like the wind through the spruce trees, and she knew he was tired. "You know how much I depend on you, Nicole," he said, touching her shoulder. "I don't want to hear any more of this foolishness."

"It's not foolishness," she said more loudly than she intended. She pulled away from him and ran up the stairs.

Annette and Babbette were in Annette's room playing records. Jimmy Rodgers' voice crooned: "It's too wonderful." It always sounded like *tits* too wonderful, *tits* too beautiful, something Nicole and Joanne always giggled over. Tonight it didn't seem funny at all. Nicole threw herself on the bed and cried.

When she came downstairs the next morning her mother had hooked up the wringer washer and was sorting a huge pile of dirty clothes. Annette was stripping the bottom sheets from the beds in the boys' room. Later, she'd put the top sheets on the bottom and fresh sheets on top. Her father stuck his head into the kitchen.

"Hurry up, Nicole," he said. "We've got to get going soon."

"I'm not going, Dad. I told you that last night." She tried to keep her voice firm and even.

"Yes you are, damn-it-all!" he yelled.

Her mother stopped sorting clothes and looked up. Annette, with her arms full of sheets, stood with her mouth open.

"No I'm not," Nicole said, buttering her toast.

"Listen," he said. "I'm going to load the truck, and you'd better be ready to go when I am or else!"

Nicole went upstairs to her room and closed the door. Her old work clothes lay on the floor where she had left them the night before. She kicked them under the bed and reached in her closet for a clean blouse. Her new blue coat shone there; next to it, everything else looked drab.

"Hey, it's me," Annette said, opening the door. "I have to get your bottom sheet. Are you really not going?"

"That's right." Nicole looked at herself in the mirror, half-combing her hair. Annette whistled under her breath.

A few minutes later Nicole heard her father coming up the stairs. His hard breathing sounded like a wind tunnel. After every few steps he paused to rest a little, his body rubbing the wall by the railing. It had been a very long time since he had come upstairs. When he got to the top he opened Nicole's door and stood there for a moment catching his breath. Except for the fringe of white hair around his head, he looked like an enormous beet.

"Why are you doing this?" he asked. "You know I need your help." His voice was gentle, half-pleading.

"Get one of the boys to help." Her own voice was high and tight. "They never do anything around here."

"André and Claude are just about useless. I have to tell them how to do every little thing. Please, Nicole, you know that Saturday is my busiest day."

"I'm too old to go with you anymore, Dad." She couldn't bear to look at him.

"Too old? Thirteen is too old?"

"Well Annette is fifteen and you don't make her go."

"Annette," her father said, shaking his head. Annette had never gone with her father in the truck. Nicole couldn't imagine her carrying boxes any more than she could imagine her mother doing it.

"Now, look, Nicole—" Her father's voice was rising. "Stop this nonsense. Get your jacket on and let's go!" His voice filled the room, and Nicole felt a hard tight spot forming in her chest. She turned toward the window and looked out over the trees.

Her mother had tiptoed up the stairs and stood in the hall beside her father. "I don't know what's gotten into that girl," he said. Her mother's forehead was wrinkled and her eyes were how they got when someone was sick. No-one said anything for a few moments.

"Well Charles, maybe it *is* time to start taking one of the boys," her mother said finally.

Her father shook his head. "Of all days. The day I go to Spryfield."

They turned and started creaking down the stairs, her father holding on to the rail with one arm, and on to her mother with the other. The thing in Nicole's chest had gotten so hard and heavy she could hardly breathe. She wanted to run downstairs and tell her father she would go, but she was held there, as if by some invisible hand. She listened to her father's breathing, his low mutterings, felt the distance between them widening with each step.

11: This Thing Between Men and Women

"He said he'd pay a dollar an hour," Claire said. "It's just for the first week in August, while Marie's on her honeymoon."

"What about the other girl?" Nicole asked. "What's-her-name."

"Oh Colleen couldn't stay alone in the house with Sam while Marie is gone. Sam's a bachelor and it wouldn't be proper. She's going home to Cape Breton, but she'll be back when Marie and her husband come back."

Sam's girls were sisters, country girls, hired to cook and clean, and help run the store.

"You mean Marie and her husband are going to live with Sam?"

"Sam said it would only be temporary, until they can find a place. Besides, Marie's husband is a sailor, so he'll be gone most of the time."

Nicole tried to imagine what it would be like: Sam, two hired girls and a sailor, all in the same house. Sam was 6'3", a lot younger than her father, but bear-shaped like him. Nicole wasn't sure she liked him. When he said, "I don't got" instead of "I don't have" little shivers ran down her back.

"Your father would be out of business if it weren't for Sam," her mother said. "Sam's a good friend to help your father and if we can help him back somehow we should."

"How is he helping Dad?" Nicole didn't discuss the business with her father anymore, not since she stopped going with him in the truck.

"Sam lent your father a lot of money this summer. The candy companies wouldn't sell to him anymore until he paid his bills. Sam's your father's partner now, though I don't think he'll make much on this investment."

All summer Sam had been coming to see her father. They'd go to the basement and talk in hushed voices. It was a lot like when the little man with round glasses used to come, except that Sam was her father's friend.

"Is Sam rich?"

"He's comfortable." Her mother pronounced the word carefully. "He has his store and his house, all paid for. And his car, a brand new 1958 Pontiac."

Nicole wanted to ask why Sam was helping her father but didn't. There was something dog-like about Sam, with his brown eyes shining behind his glasses, his swarthy complexion and his big hands covered with black hair. Once or twice a week he parked his big white Pontiac by the fire hydrant in front of their house. "I was just passing by and thought I'd drop in and say hello," he'd say, rattling the keys in his pocket and grinning at her mother like a porpoise. "Come in, come in." Her mother would brighten, hurry off her apron. "No, I can't stay," he'd say, "I'm parked in front of the hydrant."

Sometimes Sam took her mother for rides. Her mother loved to go for rides, and they never went in the truck on Sundays anymore. "That big white Pontiac rides so smoothly," her mother cooed, "it's just like riding on waves." Sometimes they stopped at Sunnyside for a lobster roll. Her mother loved lobster rolls. Once Nicole went along, just to see what it was like. It was boring.

"A dollar an hour is good pay," her mother urged. "That's as much as Annette earns."

At thirteen and three-quarters, Nicole wasn't old enough for a real job like Annette's. At fifteen, Annette could work on the city playgrounds; Nicole had to babysit a whole evening for a dollar.

"Okay, I'll do it," she said.

Her first day at Sam's store was a Friday, the day before Marie's wedding. Her father and André brought her there in the truck.

"This is a good opportunity for you, Nicole," her father said. "You can learn some valuable things about business if you pay attention." You could too, she thought. She felt angry that he had to borrow money from someone like Sam Dugas.

The truck farted and lurched down the street. Her father held the steering-wheel with both hands; his knuckles were red and puffy.

Sam's store was smaller than Nicole expected, only slightly larger than their living-room. It was, however, meticulously clean, much cleaner than any of the stores she had seen with her father on his Friday and Saturday rounds. Every item was neatly arranged on its shelf; the tile floor shone like Sam's new Pontiac.

"You work the cash register like this," Sam said, bending over her and pressing the small keys with his big fingers. He spoke with an Acadian accent like her uncles in Digby County did, thudding his th's, as if his tongue was so thick and heavy he couldn't make it do what he wanted it to do. His white shirt was open at the collar and a faint smell of spicy cologne drifted over from his neck.

"When the kids come in to buy candy, watch them," Sam said. "Sometimes they put things in their pockets"—"tings," he said, "in der pockets." He looked down at Nicole through the bottom half of his bifocals and winked, as if it were a game to catch them at it.

Nicole liked Sam more today, she decided, watching him bustle around his store, adjusting a box of macaroni that wasn't perfectly aligned with the rest.

"I got some business to take care of, I'll be back later," Sam said mid-morning, and left.

Through the partially open door that led to Sam's house Nicole could hear two female voices. She looked in now and then, curious to see the sisters, one of whom was about to marry a sailor. She could tell right away which was the bride. She was plump and had thick legs and thin, curly-permed hair. Her sister looked at her with great cow-eyes.

At noon Sam came in for a few minutes—"How are things going?"—then went back out. The bride's sister brought her an egg salad sandwich and a glass of milk. "If it gets right busy, just yell through the door and one of us will come." Her hands were large, and a film of dark hair covered her arms. Country girls, Nicole thought. When she went back into the house, she closed the door behind her.

All afternoon customers came in twos and threes. Little boys wanting a loaf of bread or a pound of baloney. Their hands hovered over the penny candy, treading the air like humming-birds. Nicole held them back with her eyes. The middle-aged women asked: "Are you the new girl?" and smiled and called her dear.

Then a man came in. He stared at her from the corners of the store until everyone else was gone.

"So," he said, leaning a tanned arm on the counter. "Sam has a new girl."

Nicole nodded.

"I'm glad he decided to get a pretty one for a change," he said, moving his eyes over her. His Rs rolled like a purr and his words were soft and padded around the edges.

Nicole leaned back on her stool and shrugged, giving him a tight smile. What could he want? Perhaps he had a gun and wanted to steal the money in her register.

"What's your name?" he asked leaning further toward her. His hair and eyes were brown like chestnuts. "Nicole," she said. "What's yours?" That way she could tell the police later if she had to.

"Steffan," he said smiling broadly, pleased that she asked. "Well little Nicole, do you have a boyfriend?"

She folded her arms in front of her chest and lied: "Yes, lots of them."

"Lots of them," he repeated, rolling his eyes. "And do you let them kiss you?" He said kiss as if it had five Ss, curling his lips forward as if he were kissing something.

"That's none of your business," Nicole said.

He threw his head back and laughed from somewhere deep in his chest. His hands, resting on the counter, had long slim fingers. Piano hands, Sister Mary Stella would call them. "Oh you're a frisky one," he said, still laughing. "I'll bet they have a good time with you."

Two old ladies came in then, followed by a girl and her younger brother. Somewhere between wrapping a soup bone for the old ladies and helping the little boy pick out five cents worth of candy, Nicole noticed that *he* was gone.

A little while later Sam appeared. "How did things go?"

"Fine." She didn't mention the man.

Annette and Babbette were in Annette's room playing records. "Kisses Sweeter Than Wine" drifted out into the hall.

Nicole knocked on the door. "Can I come in?"

"I suppose so."

Sometimes they let her in, sometimes not. They were both in their slips, and Babbette was leaning over Annette, plucking the tiny hairs from the bridge of her nose. "This is how you make your eyes look wider," she said. Annette's face was tilted up like an altar boy's. "Never never pluck above the eyebrow, though. It ruins the natural line."

Nicole studied their women's bodies. Babbette and Annette knew things. She wanted to tell them about the man in Sam's store, ask them what it meant. But she didn't quite know what to say, how to ask.

Babbette was smearing white grease all over her face now. "You should cream your face everyday," she intoned in her expert's voice. "To keep your skin soft and silky. Men like women with soft, silky skin."

The next day Sam met her at the store wearing a dark blue suit. "The reception's right after mass," he said. "They got a lunch ready." He smelled intensely of cologne and fidgeted with the cans of salmon and haddock.

The door to the house was still closed. Nicole pictured Colleen and Marie in some corner bedroom, Colleen zipping up the back of her sister's wedding dress. She wondered what it would be like to be a bride, putting on clean underwear, hooking your stockings on to your garters on the morning of your wedding.

Around noon the room behind the door flooded with thick rustlings and muffled voices. Sam popped into the store and the door drifted open behind him. Nicole caught a glimpse of Marie. Her face was pink and soft, her eyes shining. She looked almost pretty, with her white dress and lacy hat. A man stood beside her—it had to be the sailor—touching her elbow, her waist, sliding his hand up and down her back.

All afternoon the store was busy with people buying pork roasts and whole chickens for the next day's big Sunday dinner. Sam put on a big white apron and helped for a while, then went back into the house.

"Did you see Marie?" her mother asked when she got home.

"Yes," Nicole said. "She looked nice."

"Sam dropped by for a minute after they'd all gone. He told me it went well."

Nicole pictured Sam leaning over her mother in the doorway, the corners of his thick mouth fluttering foolishly. When her father came home, her mother didn't mention that Sam stopped by.

On Monday afternoon the store was quiet. Around four, *he* came in. He studied the labels on the soup cans until the woman with the two children left; then he came to the counter.

"And how is my pretty little Nicole today?" he asked.

"I'm just fine," she answered. "But I'm not *your* little anything."

"Oh but I wish you were," he said, leaning so far over the counter that she could feel his breath. She was suddenly aware that there was no-one home next door.

"You'd be so much more fun than the girl I was with Saturday night." He looked at her smiling, inviting her to ask.

"Oh?" Nicole tried not to look too interested.

"She's twenty, fiery like you but not as sweet." He said sweet the way he said kiss the time before, holding the word in his mouth like a piece of hard candy. "She was nice for a while, but then she bit me." He pointed to a bluish mark on his bottom lip. "Can you imagine that?"

This struck Nicole as enormously funny. She started to laugh.

"You wouldn't do that though, would you?"

She couldn't stop laughing. She looked at the blue mark on

his lip and laughter rippled up and down her spine, her legs.

"Would you?" His left eyebrow arched into a question mark.

At six, Sam closed the store for a while to take her home. "It's not very busy on Monday nights," he said. The inside of the Pontiac was red and smelled of leather. Music bubbled softly from the radio and everything felt hushed and cozy, like the inside of a confessional.

"So how do you like working in the store?" Sam asked.

"I like it fine. You were right about the little boys, though."

"What do you mean?"

"Their hands. You have to watch their hands."

Sam laughed. His mouth fell open and his whole body jiggled.

"Your mother told me you'd be a good worker and she was right." He looked at her out of the corner of his eye to see her reaction. Nicole thought of her mother, sitting where she was sitting, next to Sam in all this cozy redness. It seemed different from the time she'd gone with them.

"My mother really likes your car," she told Sam. "She likes it when you take her for rides."

Sam's mouth twitched with pleasure. "A woman as beautiful as your mother deserves some fun now and then. She's a good woman to stand by your father during all his troubles." Nicole pictured her mother standing by her father. Then she pictured her riding in the big white Pontiac, her voice tinkling like little bells.

All week was the same. In the late afternoon when Sam wasn't there, *he* appeared. When people came in he went to the shelves and examined labels; after they left he leaned on the counter and told her things. "Your eyes are the colour of chicory flowers. And your skin, so white, so delicious." He showed her the pink tip of his tongue. Part of her wished he wouldn't come. Part of her waited for him.

"What are you going to do with all your money?" Annette asked. All summer, Annette had been buying herself lipsticks, and scarves. She dabbed some "Evening in Paris" behind her ear.

"I don't know yet."

Friday was her last day at the store. All day she felt restless and queer. Marie and her husband were back—Marie came into the store to get a bottle of Javex and a loaf of bread. Nicole watched her move around, bend and reach for things. The body of a new bride.

Around four o'clock, *he* appeared. She pretended not to notice him standing by the pop case watching her. "We could go for a ride tomorrow night," he whispered. "We could go to Citadel Hill and watch the sunset." He looked at her the way Sam looked at her mother, as if she were a prize he wanted to win.

"I don't think so," she said. She had a sudden urge to tell him: I'm only thirteen and three-quarters.

"That's so sad," he said, the Ss curling out of his mouth like steam.

Just before closing time, Sam counted out $56.00 into her hand. "Make sure you keep it somewhere safe," he said, winking. "I'll drive you home, though, just in case." Nicole had never had so much money all at once. She folded it and put it in her purse.

Outside, dense fingers of fog were rolling in from the harbour.

"It'll be thick like chowder by nine," Sam said. "We'll hear the foghorns for sure tonight."

They turned onto Robie Street, and stopped for a light. Two sailors, each holding a woman by the hand, crossed in front of them. One of the sailors put his arm around the woman's shoulders and she leaned into him.

Tomorrow, when *he* came to the store, he would find her gone. He would wait by the meat case, pretending to study its contents, and wonder if she was in the back room somewhere. A few days later, he would remark to Marie or Colleen, "That other one, doesn't she work here anymore?" "No," they would tell him. "She was only temporary." He would not ask where she lived, and they would not tell him.

The street lights blinked on suddenly, and the fog wrapped itself around them until they were muffled and dim, like secrets.

She could have asked him for things, and he would have given them to her.

12: Influences

Nicole wasn't sure she wanted to go to a Convent school. There were no boys there, and she didn't know anyone.

"Look, all I ask is that you take the examinations. There's no guarantee you'll win."

"Did Annette take the exams when she was in grade 8?"

"No," Claire said. "She had other ideas." When Annette was in grade 8, Claire had badgered her for months about it. It was such a good opportunity—a full scholarship to the prestigious Convent of the Sacred Heart. Each year they offered one to a promising grade 8 girl whose parents could otherwise not afford to send her. But Annette had refused to take the exams. By then she had the body of a full-grown woman, and would not even consider going to a high school without boys. Annette had once been so smart. Now she didn't care at all about school.

If only she could have sent Annette there, with or without a scholarship, Claire thought. But even with her full-time teacher's salary, they still found it hard to make ends meet. She needed to make her daughters see how important education was. Where would they be now, if it weren't for *her* education?

"You and Annette are not the same," she continued. "You're different. You have a chance to be somebody."

Nicole wasn't sure she wanted to be different. She wanted to be like everyone else. Everyone else would be going to St. Pat's.

"Why is Sacred Heart better than St. Pat's?"

Her mother made a snorting sound. "Anyone can go to St Pat's. Wild kids from all over the city go there. There are all sorts of bad influences." If Annette had gone to the Convent

School she would have met nice girls. She wouldn't be sneaking around all the time with that Babbette.

"Sacred Heart has high standards," she continued. "Many of the girls go on to college. You'd meet the right kind of people there." She thought of the wide lawns of the Convent grounds, the cultivated voices of the nuns she had talked to. Dr. McLean sent his daughters there. So did many of the prosperous professional people from the South End.

Nicole wasn't sure about "the right kind of people," but she agreed, finally, to take the exams. She wouldn't win anyway, she told herself, and taking the exams would make her mother happy.

She didn't think about the Convent School again until early June when the letter came. A few days later, her picture appeared in the paper. The teachers at St. Catherine's School beamed at her, told her they were proud. But the kids, except for Joanne, began giving her strange looks, as if they didn't know her.

Everything was changing, and Nicole wasn't sure she liked this. She'd started her period a few months before and her breasts were finally growing. But now it didn't seem like such a big deal. In fact the monthlies made her ill. Soon, everyone would be starting high school. And everyone except her would be going to St. Pat's.

Even Annette was changing. She didn't talk to Nicole much anymore. She and Babbette were always going some place, meeting boys. Tonight they were getting ready to go to a Knights of Columbus dance. They went out to dances almost every Friday and Saturday now, sometimes by themselves, sometimes with dates. Nicole had never gone out with a boy. She wondered if she would ever get to, now that she was going to go to an all-girls school.

Annette and Babbette were rubbing their legs with a depilatory mitt, making circles in time to an Everly Brothers song.

"Having beautiful legs is really important," Babbette was saying. "Men like women with beautiful legs. I read an article about it in *Chatelaine*. It's all in the calf muscles; if your calf muscles are well-developed and in the right place, you'll have beautiful legs." She held up her right leg and admired it.

"What are you wearing tonight?" Nicole asked Annette. Annette had a summer job clerking at Zeller's and was buying herself fancy new dresses all the time.

"My red," Annette said.

Annette's red dress followed all the curves of her body and the little cup sleeves teetered provocatively on her shoulders. Though she had just turned sixteen, Annette looked at least eighteen when she wore that dress.

"Didn't you wear your red to the KC dance last Saturday?" Nicole asked.

"So what?" Annette said stiffening slightly.

"I'll bet you're really going to the Jubilee," Nicole said. She kept her voice low and confidential, so they'd know she could be trusted. Annette was forbidden to go to the Jubilee, but she and Babbette went anyway. Sailors went there, and people smoked and drank. And you were supposed to be eighteen.

Annette looked at her narrowly. "If I tell you, will you promise not to tell Mom?"

"The Madames of the Sacred Heart are a French order," her mother said. "And cultured. The nuns are all from good families and well educated. They all know how to speak French."

Her mother talked about the Convent School all the time now. It was as if *she* had won the scholarship.

"That's one of the nice things about going there. It'll help you keep your French. You'll learn to read and write it. It's a shame when Acadian children lose their French." She gave André a hard look. This past year he had begun calling himself Andy. Whenever she heard his friends call him that she'd say angrily, "His name is André. Can't you say that? It isn't so hard."

Nicole was still not sure what she thought about it all. On the one hand, it was nice to feel celebrated. People she barely knew still approached her after Mass to offer congratulations. Even her father seemed happy about it. After she stopped going with him in the truck, he seemed not to notice her very much. Now he looked at her differently, as if there were something special about her he hadn't noticed before.

But Joanne would be going to St Pat's. And Annette and Babbette and all their friends went there. Nicole was afraid she would miss something.

When school started, Nicole felt nervous and queer. She and Joanne rode the bus together as far as Oxford Street. Then Joanne and Annette and Babbette and half the other passengers got off to transfer to another bus—the one going to St. Pat's. Nicole watched them all cross the street. Joanne turned and waved goodbye, and a hard lump formed in Nicole's throat. She felt, suddenly, as if they were saying goodbye forever.

Her mother had told her how "genteel" and "cultured" the Convent School was, but the old brick building with its steeples and gables struck her as odd and old-fashioned. A high wrought-iron fence surrounded manicured grounds with long hedge rows and flowerbeds tucked in unexpected places. Paths led to small shrines with statues of the Infant Jesus or Our Lady, with places to kneel and say the rosary. Everything seemed hushed and mysterious: it reminded Nicole of her favourite childhood book, *The Secret Garden*. The nuns, who were cloistered and confined to the building and grounds, were called "Mother," instead of "Sister."

The basement cloakroom was full of girls, some looking awkward and overly eager. New girls, Nicole thought. Is that how she looked? The old girls knew right away where to put their sweaters and jackets, and where the bathrooms were. They all wore the same dark blue uniforms with light blue blouses and brown oxfords. She scanned their faces for something familiar, some clue that one of these girls might become her friend.

Upstairs, the floor boards in the corridors creaked; pictures of girls in white dresses with blue satin sashes hung from the walls; long brown cords holding dim lights dangled from high ceilings. Yet everything seemed oddly cheerful. The nuns all smiled and hugged the old girls as they came in; everyone looked happy, as if they all liked being there.

In study hall they were assigned places. Their desks, old and rickety with lids that lifted, held large cubicles for their books and pencils and white gloves. Mother Johnson called out the names of the First Academic class. When her name was called, Nicole felt a sudden, odd sensation, as if she had just found herself in a safe, familiar place. Yet this was her first time here.

When they filed into their classrooms, Mother Murphy, their homeroom teacher, called out their names again. Again, Nicole felt the same small jolt of recognition she had felt before. It was as if they all knew her, and liked her. It was her name, she realized suddenly. The way Mother Murphy and Mother Johnson said it—with a short o, "Ni-cull," the way her mother and father and aunts and uncles said it. The French way. Everyone else she knew called her "Ni-call" or "Ni-coal."

In each class they were given books: Classics. Latin. Theology instead of Cathecism. English Literature. It was all fascinating and exciting and a bit frightening. Would she be able to learn all that? Would they expect more of her because she was the scholarship student? Every time they said her name, she relaxed a bit.

The last period was French. Their teacher, Mother McGuire, was short and square with small, round glasses, and a pink, cheery face. She bobbed around the room like an eager robin. "French is what we call a Romance language," she said. "So are Italian, Spanish and Portuguese, to name a few. Can anyone tell me why these languages are called Romance languages?"

A few titters rose from the class, but no-one raised a hand.

"Meredith, what do you think?"

Meredith was one of the new girls. "Um, well, could it be that men from those countries—aren't they supposed to be, um, more romantic than other men?"

"That may be so, dear; I'm sure I wouldn't know." Wild laughter erupted from the class. Meredith turned dark red, and shrank into her chair.

"When it comes to languages, 'Romance' means something else. What word does it sound like? One that begins with capital R?"

Gillian from the back row raised her hand. "Isn't it from Rome, or Roman? French comes from Latin, doesn't it? That's what the Romans spoke."

"You are absolutely right, my dear. All the Romance languages derive from Latin, the language of the Romans."

Gillian beamed, and everyone looked at her enviously. Gillian was an old girl.

"Let's start by seeing how many French words you already know," Mother McGuire continued.

Nicole sat up straight. This was her chance to prove herself. She still spoke some French with her aunts and uncles when they visited Digby County in the summer. Few of the other girls, she noticed, had Acadian names.

"Does anyone know how to say, 'Good day?'"

Nicole shot her hand up, but Mother McGuire called on Gay.

"Bonjour," Gay said, and Mother McGuire rewarded her with a big smile. "Now, does anyone know how to say, 'How are you?'"

Nicole waved her hand hard.

"Nicole," Mother McGuire said.

"Comment ça va?" Nicole said, aware that every one was looking at her.

"Well, yes, that's correct," Mother McGuire said, but she looked a bit doubtful. "You should use the 'vous' form, though: 'Comment allez vous.' It's much more polite than addressing people with the familiar 'tu.'" She turned to the board and wrote "vous" and "tu". "Except among very close friends, always use 'vous' when addressing others."

Nicole felt, suddenly, as if she had said something rude. In Digby County they always said "tu" for you. She'd thought the "vous" only meant plural.

Mother McGuire went on asking more questions but Nicole didn't raise her hand. When she asked, "Can anyone say, 'The car is here?'" Nicole put up her hand again. That one had nothing about tu or vous in it.

Mother McGuire nodded, and Nicole said, "Le char est icite."

Mother McGuire winced. "Well, dear, that's country French. The proper way to say it is, 'L'auto est ici.' We're going to learn only good French here."

Nicole felt her face get hot and she willed herself to become invisible. When the bell finally rang, she hurried to get her jacket and ran to the bus without speaking to anyone.

At supper, she told her mother what had happened.

"Well she's wrong!" her mother said. "It's not bad French. It's *old* French. Our ancestors came from France early in the seventeenth century. Words like char and icite were the words they used in France then. The language changed, but the Acadians were isolated, so they spoke the old way. It's perfectly good French."

Nicole wasn't sure about this. When Mother McGuire said French words, they sounded like high, thin violins. When her aunts and uncles said them, they sound like fiddles twanging.

"Imagine her saying it was bad French! She should know better! She's not French herself, remember that. She doesn't know everything."

The next day, when Nicole went into Study Hall, she felt nervous. Would they think of her as some ignorant country girl? She looked out of the corner of her eye to see if anyone was laughing at her. A few of the old girls from the South End came in giggling, but they didn't look her way.

In the corridor on the way to class, Meredith came up behind her and said, "Hi Nicole." She pronounced Nicole's name the way the nuns had the day before. Nicole had never had a friend who said her name right. Even Joanne called her "Ni-call." She remembered Meredith in class yesterday. How red she had turned. When they went to homeroom, they sat together.

Annette had a new boyfriend. Nicole sat on the front steps waiting to see what he looked like. He wasn't a boy from St. Pat's, she'd told Nicole. He was Lebanese, and he was through with school. She had met him at a dance, though she wouldn't say where. Nicole suspected it was the Jubilee. Finally, their mother told Annette she had to bring him home to meet them. That was the proper way to do things, she'd said.

Her father was fiddling with the lock on the back door of

the truck. A few nights before, a thief had tried to break it open while he was parked on Robie Street. André, sitting in the front, had yelled, scaring the thief away. Now the padlock wouldn't close quite right.

A white half-ton truck, a lot like her father's but newer, pulled up in front of the house. A tall, slim man stepped out dressed in a dark suit and tie. Something about his big square jaw, his dark oiled hair piled high over his forehead, made him look important.

He went over to her father and said his name. Her father said: "Well, so it's you," and shook his hand. He kept smiling at the man with a peculiar smile and shifting from one foot to the other. Nicole couldn't figure it out. Her father wasn't expecting anyone, but she didn't think a grown man would be coming for Annette. In a few moments Annette came bouncing down the steps, her pony tail and breasts bobbing, the sleeves of her red dress half falling off her shoulders.

Their mother stood at the door watching. After they left, she went down to the truck. "He's much too old for her!" she snapped.

"He's a good man," her father said. "I've seen him around. He and his brothers have a novelty business. He works hard; he could provide for her."

"Provide for her!" her mother hissed. "She's only sixteen!"

The next morning when Annette came down for breakfast the fights started.

13: Saturday Night

Annette stood at the ironing-board, ironing the dress she planned to wear that night. Claire, folding a basket of laundry at the kitchen table, kept looking over at her, her mouth tightening. Nicole tried to hurry up and finish the dishes; she knew what was coming.

"You'll ruin your life this way," Claire said in a low voice.

Annette's shoulders stiffened but she kept ironing.

"Eleven years older is too old. You have no idea what it means to live with an older man. Oh, it seems nice at first, 'romantic.' Then they get old and sick and don't care anymore. Wait 'till you see how romantic that is." Her mother's eyes were burning into points.

Any minute, now, Nicole thought.

"I'm only trying to help you, Annette, to give you the benefit of my experience, but will you listen? No. You think you know everything."

Suddenly Annette turned and hissed: "It's *my* life, not yours!" Her mother's face swelled up as if she'd been slapped and words flew through the air like sharpened teeth. "Miss Smart Alec—" "None of your business—" "You little fool—"

Nicole slipped out the back door and went around to the front porch to wait it out. At first she had watched them, fascinated. They were like the cats—Minou or Solomon with Midnight next door, crouching along the fence line, singing their high-pitched taunts like arias. When one of them went too far the other would be on her in a frenzy of shrieks and hisses.

But these fights had been going on for over a year. And they weren't funny anymore. An invisible wall had sprung up in their house, with Annette and their father on one side, their mother on the other. Nicole wanted to stay neutral, like the boys, who always seemed to be out somewhere when things got sticky.

She listened at the front door. Footsteps hurried up the stairs, Annette's voice shouted: "I don't care what anyone thinks! I'm going to marry Emile next summer when I turn eighteen, whether you like it or not!" A door slammed.

Nicole wasn't sure how she felt about the Annette-Emile business. She liked Emile, but since he'd come along, Annette had changed. She seemed to have gotten smaller, quieter; now all she ever talked about was Emile and getting married.

Last spring when Annette announced that she was quitting school now that she had her grade 11, her mother had exploded. Her father said nothing. It didn't seem to bother him at all. And though the battles had raged all summer, Annette hadn't gone back to St. Pat's. Instead, when school started a few weeks ago, she just kept working at Zeller's. Sometimes she worked in housewares, sometimes in the candy section. Nicole and Meredith had dropped in to see her one afternoon after school. In her brown uniform, standing behind the counter with all the other girls, Annette had looked so ordinary that it took a while before Nicole recognized her.

When the house was completely quiet, Nicole tiptoed up the stairs to her room, pausing at Annette's closed door. She could hear Annette moving around, getting ready. And very low, so low she had to strain to hear it, the sound of the Everly brothers, their voices twanging from Annette's small record player: "...never knew what I missed, till I kissed you...."

From her bedroom window, Nicole watched Emile get out of his car. He wore a freshly pressed dark suit, as he always did, and walked up the front steps briskly, confidently, as if he owned all of Halifax. When he stood in the front hall twirling his keys and waiting for Annette, Nicole sat halfway down the stairs studying his broad jaw, his white teeth, his wave of oiled black hair. When he saw Nicole, his mouth stretched into a big smile, and he began his usual banter, asking her if she had any boyfriends yet, as if she were still a child. This past year she'd gone to a few dances at Saint Mary's Boys Academy with Meredith and some of the other Convent girls, but she wasn't about to tell Emile that.

"I'm almost as old as Annette was when she started going out with *you*," she said, giving him a saucy smile.

He put his hand to his chest and gestured extravagantly, as if he had just made a breathtaking discovery. "In that case," he said, drawing the words out importantly, "We'll just have to find you a Lebanese boyfriend. I have several cousins who would like to go out with a nice, pretty girl like you. How would you like that? We could all go out together, your sister and I, and you and my cousin, who would be so happy and pleased."

Nicole wondered if his cousins would look like him, or the man that summer in Sam's store. But Emile practically crooned the words, so Nicole knew he was just teasing. This was the same tone of voice he used when he told her mother how nice she looked, even if she was wearing an old house-dress. He'd say, "You and Annette look more like sisters than mother and daughter." Her mother would smile and flutter her eyes, but when Emile and Annette left, she'd tell Nicole, "The Lebanese are all like that; they don't really mean what they say."

Just as Annette and Emile were about to leave, her father appeared, dressed in his Sunday suit. His face glowed bright pink from his bath, and his neck smelled of Bay Rum. His fringe of white hair was carefully combed.

"Can you drop me off at St. Catherine's on the way?" he asked Emile. "There's no place to park my truck, and climbing that hill is hard on my arthritis." Her father went to confession once a month, on a Saturday evening.

"I'd be glad to, Mr. LeBlanc," Emile said, no longer crooning. When he talked to her father, his voice sounded different, as if they shared a secret, something men knew but women didn't.

Nicole's mother came to the door, and they watched the threesome walk down the front steps and get into Emile's car. Her father lifted his legs slowly and eased himself in. They stood at the door for a few minutes, looking out. Then her mother sighed. "What do *you* think? Should I give them my permission and let them get married?"

"I don't know," Nicole answered, looking down. "Your father thinks we should let her," her mother continued. "He says Emile's a fine man and there's no reason to stop them. Of course your father doesn't see anything wrong with anything as long as it doesn't affect him. But seventeen is so young. She needs to meet other people."

"Annette's been going out with Emile for a long time," Nicole said, picking her words carefully. "Even if you don't let them get married, that doesn't mean she'll meet anyone else."

Her mother thought about this for a moment.

"I hope you won't be as foolish as your sister," she said, giving her a hard look.

A few hours later, Claire found herself alone, the evening stretching before her like an empty, flat road. She turned on the TV. Ralph and Alice were yelling at each other in a way that sounded too familiar, so she shut them off and went into the kitchen.

The crossword puzzle she had torn out of the paper earlier lay on the counter. She picked it up and found a pencil. Across, 1: a six-letter word meaning a person who does heavy work. That was easy: drudge. She thought for a moment, then pencilled in: C-L-A-I-R-E. She looked around at the wringer washer by the sink that had sloshed through eight loads of wash that morning, at the oil stove whose surface she had scrubbed with steel wool, at the pies she had baked—one apple, one lemon meringue (they had eaten the cherry for supper). Two baskets of clothes waited under the ironing board.

She sat back in her chair and sighed. Maybe she would go up to her room and read for a while.

She felt tired, yes; but that wasn't it, exactly. She kept thinking of Annette and Emile. They were going to the Jubilee. She had never been there but imagined a jolly crowd making jokes, having a good time—a crowd like those at the dances she had gone to as a rural schoolteacher. They'd be better dressed at the Jubilee of course, and couples could step outside and watch the lights reflecting on the Northwest Arm, but otherwise, it would be the same.

Almost every Saturday night there had been a dance somewhere, at the legion hall or church basement of some village near where she taught. She and other young women from the village would walk there in pairs; or, laughing and waving their dancing shoes, hitch a ride from a passing waggon or car. How she had loved dancing! The Jitterbug, the Foxtrot, the Virginia Reel—she knew how to do them all. During the slow dances, couples would drift to the dim corners, say secret things with their eyes, lips, hands. Suddenly, her limbs ached to be held, to move rhythmically to some sweet music. Would she never have that again in her life?

A series of sharp cracking sounds drew her to the window. After finding a packet of Black Cats stuffed inside one of Claude's winter boots, she had expressly forbidden the boys to play with firecrackers. Not only were they dangerous, they were illegal, even though all the neighbourhood boys seemed to have them. She scanned the area by Mr. Penny's garage, the bushes by the McKenzies, the hollow area behind the Smiths' front steps. No sign of André and Claude. But something else caught her eye—a white Pontiac moving slowly down the street. She drew her breath sharply and stepped back to the side of the window.

Would he dare come to the door again? She felt herself prickle with curiosity and indignation.

If only things hadn't gotten so out of hand.

At first she had found it lovely to go for a ride now and then, to have someone to talk to. He seemed to understand, and she found his attentions flattering. All last year he had appeared sporadically at the door of the teachers' lounge at noon, surprising her with a chunky roll bulging with lobster salad, or a large order of hot clams and chips. Though it pleased her—what he brought was much tastier than the cold baloney sandwich she usually had in her bag—she knew the other teachers whispered about it among themselves.

It's not what you think, she wanted to tell them. He's just a friend. A friend of my husband's.

And when he began waiting in the schoolyard two or three times a week to drive her home, his gleaming white Pontiac difficult to ignore, the other teachers said: Your chauffeur is here, and hid their smiles.

By the end of the school year, the whole thing had become a bit tiresome. She had begun to notice his tendency to say the same things over and over, and his chronic bad grammar made her wince. By the middle of the summer, what had once seemed a pleasant diversion now seemed not worth the effort. So she told him to stop coming, that people were talking. He cried and told her he loved her. He couldn't bear not seeing her, he said; she couldn't drive him away, it would kill him.

His response had shocked her. She had let him kiss her a few times, during moments of weakness, when they were watching the sunset over the Bedford Basin, or listening to the pounding waves at Peggy's Cove—but that was all. It hadn't seemed like much; he had been so good to them, lending Charles money that he couldn't possibly hope to get back. But she hadn't promised him anything. And what did he think, after all. He wasn't the sort of man she would take seriously even if she were free, which she wasn't. Poor Sam. If only he hadn't misunderstood how things were.

She watched the car pause in front of the fire hydrant. Would he stop?

This past month he had come by twice pretending to look for Charles. She had been polite but cool: Charles isn't here right now, but I'll tell him you came by. It embarrassed her to see him, that hangdog look, that forlorn, quivering mouth. Was she going to have to go through all that again? She pictured him standing at the door. He would suggest they go for a ride, pehaps to Sunnyside one last time before it closed for the winter. It was a lovely evening, too, the kind of evening when she used to look forward to a ride. Maybe if he promised not to carry on...

But the white car paused only for a moment, then glided silently down the street.

"It's just as well," she said aloud. And yet she felt seized by loneliness. Over the rooftops a few streaks of pink and orange lingered in the half dark. It had been a beautiful September day, crisp as a ripe apple, and now it was ending. Everything was blazing—the sky, the trees. Soon winter would come, with all its white stillness. I'm still young! she wanted to shout to the sky.

14: Yellow Moon

"I just need a little cash to tide me over," Charles explained.

"You know I don't have any to spare," Claire said.

"Damn it, Claire, I'm only asking for a little help." She wouldn't even look at him. She kept her eyes on the magazine she was reading.

"I'm sorry, Charles, but you need to manage your own affairs," she said. "If I give you my money it will disappear like all the rest. One of us has to be able to keep a roof over our heads."

She used her salary to pay the mortgage and buy things for herself and the children, but he was almost certain she kept a nest egg somewhere.

"Manage my own affairs," he grumbled. "That's what I'm trying to do, in spite of my poor health, and when I ask you for a little help, you refuse. That's a fine thing for a wife to do."

Claire picked up her magazine and went upstairs to her room. They had had this conversation before; it always ended this way.

He shuffled down to the basement and fingered the stack of letters on his desk. Money, money—they all wanted money. He examined a bill from McCormick. He had bought the goods more than a year ago and long since sold them. Where *had* all the money gone? Wherever it was that money went, he supposed. It was always the same. McCormick had begun shipping everything COD now, which meant he had to pay all the freight charges as well. Ganong had recently stopped selling to him, period. He owed them...how much was it? The tone in their letters was growing increasingly demanding.

Somehow he had to get hold of some cash to pay off a few bills before all the candy companies stopped selling to him. He didn't dare approach Sam again, since he hadn't paid back much of the old loan from almost two years ago. Sam hadn't mentioned it in a while; better not remind him.

Perhaps COD was best after all, even if he did have to pay for the freight. At least those shipments were paid for. It meant, though, that he could buy fewer goods.

He took off his glasses and rubbed his eyes. If only his body didn't ache all the time! Maybe he could keep track of things better. When Nicole helped him, it had all seemed easier. She knew where things were, paid attention. If only the boys could be more helpful. But at twelve and fourteen, Claude and André seemed more interested in mischief. Claude especially. Behind that innocent face with its pink baby-cheeks lurked the mind of a prankster. He and André ran in a pack, like dogs, and Claude was always full of ideas. He'd hear them scheming: how funny it would be to tie up the legs of all the longjohns on the clotheslines up and down the street, or hide behind the bushes and make rude noises while Doreen Smith kissed her boyfriend goodnight.

Though they took turns helping out after school and on weekends, they spent half the time pestering him to buy them hotdogs or fish and chips. And where were they now when he needed them to help load the truck? They had disappeared right after supper. He suspected what they were up to, too. These crisp, Indian summer evenings were perfect for prowling, and he'd been hearing firecrackers almost every night. He'd warned them over and over about firecrackers. In fact, he found himself raging at them constantly these days. Hot angers flew through him, made him want to shake them, to hit them, but they escaped like slippery eels and the anger passed. Just last night he'd been trying to read the paper when they came running through the living-room, banging into the furniture, making a huge racket. Though he yelled at them, they continued their roughhousing, and he found himself lunging for them as they fled through the back door. Afterwards, he'd felt foolish. They were just boys, after all, full of energy and spirit. You couldn't expect too much from them.

He put his glasses back on and walked over to the drainage ditch to urinate. Claire never came downstairs anymore; she'd never know the difference.

The basement had become increasingly shabby. Here and there along the shelves were half-opened boxes of failed experiments, like the altarboy and angel candles left over from last Christmas. He hadn't even recouped his investment, and now they were too faded or chipped or melted to try selling again this year. His once-large inventory was dwindling to a modest supply of things that sold well and assorted piles of odds and ends that wouldn't sell at all.

If only he could stop. If only he could put it all behind him, forget about it, rest. But these letters, they had to be answered. He picked up his fountain pen and stared at a blank piece of stationery. What could he tell them? Wait a little longer, I'll find the money somewhere? Somehow, he couldn't pull the words out. Maybe he could answer them on Sunday afternoon, after his nap, when he felt rested. He'd think of something to tell them then.

He got up from his desk and looked at the truck. Well he wasn't going to wait around for the boys to come home. He'd get them up an hour earlier in the morning; they could load up then.

Just before he started up the stairs, he heard the cats shrieking outside. He went to the basement door and called: "Here puss, puss, puss." They were down to four now, Minou and three young toms. Every few years a wave of distemper swept through the neighbourhood and killed off a third to a half of the cat population. Six months later, a new batch of young ones replaced them. Minou had escaped the last few outbreaks, but didn't contribute to the repopulation. Something had gone wrong that time in the attic; she'd had no babies since then.

He called again, more loudly, but none of the cats appeared. An enormous moon lit up the sky. No wonder the cats were so wild. Every night this week he'd heard them squalling under his window. The toms, Blackie, Putty and Solomon Three (so named because he was orange like the other two Solomons before him), came home with bloody ears, and tufts of fur missing. Even sweet little Minou, who had to be five or six years old by now, slept all day and refused to come in at night.

The moon, huge and reddish yellow, stared out from the night like an enormous eye. He'd seen an October moon like that once before, he remembered now. When he was still a young man living in Cape Breton. The whole village had talked about it for years because of the winter that came after. Huge ice floes had choked the harbour for months; coal, wood and food supplies gave out, and several people died. It was that October moon, people said.

The next morning Charles woke at 6.30 AM. He had been rising early for so many years that his body no longer required an alarm. He looked in on the boys, still wrapped in a hard sleep. André, in the top bunk, had slung an arm out; it dangled over the side strangely, like a dismembered limb. Claude, below, slept slack-jawed, drooling into the pillow. They looked so young sleeping there, like little boys still. It was André's turn to go with him today. A tuft of coarse brown hair hung over his forehead and his eyelids quivered in dream. He wouldn't wake him just yet.

He put a pot of coffee on to boil and went to see about the cats. They'd be hungry after their big night on the prowl. He opened the back door and looked out. The moon, though smaller, paler, still hung in the sky like a sentry.

By the time the truck was loaded and they were on their way, it was a little past nine. It was a beautiful, still day, the sun glinting off the maples like red gold. Charles felt his spirits rise. The Spryfield-Herring Cove route was always a good one. He could usually count on as many sales today as on two or three weekdays put together. Maybe tomorrow when he wrote to the candy companies, he could send along a few small cheques.

The first two stops were fairly routine. A few cartons of chips, a few boxes of assorted penny candy. His larger customers were farther down the road. Paul Pettipas would probably have a good order today, since his order last week had been small.

When they arrived at his store, however, Pettipas told him, "I'll have four cartons of chips and two boxes of Double Bubble gum."

"What about penny candy?" "I've decided not to stock it anymore," he said. "It just doesn't sell like it used to. I have to stock what will sell." He gave Charles an apologetic look.

Charles could see for himself that the boxes of wild cherries and chocolate buds and spearmint leaves on Pettipas' candy shelf were not even half empty. Pettipas had moved them over to one side and expanded his candy bar display. There were at least twenty different kinds there now. It shouldn't have surprised him, he thought. More and more, he was seeing penny candy being replaced by candy bars and bag candy. "That makes it hard on the small wholesalers," Charles said. "Neilson and Cadbury won't sell to us."

"Dad, can we get some donuts?" André tugged at his arm. Coconut, chocolate and glazed donuts, all freshly made, glistened on a tray by the cash register.

"Don't start on that," he said. "We just finished breakfast a little while ago. Bring in Mr. Pettipas' order."

"Things aren't too good these days for any small business," Pettipas said. "With that big new IGA store they built we're all losing customers. It's bad all over."

"You're right about that," Charles said, remembering the bills on his desk at home.

"Maloney, down the road, told me he might have to close down," Pettipas said.

"Maloney? He's been there since I started coming to Spryfield." A few years back, both Maloney and Pettipas had been good for at least a dozen boxes of penny candy every week.

"I know. But his store is small, and people just aren't shopping there any more. They want to go where there's six of everything to choose from." He shook his head in disgust. "That big IGA is hurting us all."

André brought in the chips and gum and stood by the counter, looking longingly at the donuts. Though he ate constantly, he was bone thin.

"Just one, Dad? Please?"

"Well, all right." It wasn't André's fault that business was bad. Maybe he'd have one himself. He could use a little pick-me-up right now.

By the time they got home it was after six and Charles was exhausted. His back hurt, his hands were tight and swollen, and his legs felt like dead weights. After supper, Claire and the girls went upstairs and Charles settled in his chair by the radio. He heard the boys go out the back door. Now, if Claire and Annette didn't start in on one another, maybe he could have an evening of peace and quiet. The whole upstairs had become a forbidden zone: all those females with their quarrels and secrets. He and the boys knew better than to go up there.

But everything seemed peaceful tonight. First, Annette came down calm and cheerful, saying she was going over to Babbette's for a while, that Emile would pick her up there. Then Claire came down all powdered and lipsticked, her dark, glossy hair freshly brushed. She had on a black skirt and a shimmery blouse he hadn't remembered seeing before.

"Are you going somewhere?" he asked.

"Yes," she said, walking toward the coat rack. Then, as if remembering something, she paused and said, "Annie Ryan, one of the teachers from school, asked me if I would go see *The Student Prince* with her. It's playing at the Capitol."

She looked pretty, a little flushed and excited.

"You look nice," he said, offering her a smile.

"We might go somewhere for a piece of pie afterwards," she added, not looking at him.

"Fine," he said. With everyone gone, he could listen to his opera records without interruption and doze in his chair.

It's as if they know, Claire thought, looking at the other passengers on the bus. The old woman with the dour face and the pancake-like hat kept staring at her. Even the bus driver looked at her suspiciously. And that man across the aisle— what if she saw him there? Would he remember seeing her on the bus, holding her purse and gloves so nervously?

You need a little fun in your life, Annie had told her, or you'll just shrivel up like a hard old woman.

She thought of all the stories Annie told. All her boyfriends, all the mischief she got into. It was this carefreeness, this passion for fun that had attracted Claire to Annie. The other teachers, too, talked about the dances, Church suppers, the movies they went to on Saturday night with their husbands and boyfriends. Everyone went out. Everyone except *her*. She turned toward the window. A hard, angry face looked back. She looked away and tried to soften her expression. Annie was right. An evening out would do her some good.

If only she didn't feel so queer. She hadn't felt this way with Sam. But then, he was the one who started coming around, insisting on taking her places. She really hadn't done anything to encourage him. Going out this way, though, seemed, well, different.

That young couple over there—were they talking about her?

She leaned into the window, past her reflection, and stared at the rows of quiet houses. If she were home now, she'd be watching television, or ironing—another boring, leaden evening. And Charles would be complaining about his aches and pains. It was partly his own fault that he felt so bad. He needed to lose weight, to lower his blood pressure; then he'd feel better and have more energy. But every night he piled his plate up and smothered everything with salt and gravy. She thought of him crumpled in his chair, telling her how nice she looked. She felt a sudden surge of pity for him. It wasn't all his fault; he couldn't help getting old.

Over the rooftops there was a sudden explosion of light—the moon appeared from behind a thin veil of cloud. Glorious and yellow, it filled the sky. Claire felt a thrill pass through her. All at once the moonlit evenings of her young womanhood teased her memory like a tantalizing perfume. People always said there was a man in the moon and searched for his face. But anyone could see that the moon was female, round and mysterious, like a woman on her way to a dance.

The Newfoundland Club, a cinderblock hall with a raised platform at one end and a small kitchen and cloakroom at the other, teemed with people. Tables and chairs skirted a large wooden dance floor. "During the week, they use this place for Bingo," Annie said, steering Claire around the room. "What a change, eh?"

Annie was a Newfoundlander and as a club member, could bring guests. There were several groups like that; the Cape Bretoners had their own club, too. Claire had never heard of an Acadian club and thought how nice it would be if they had one. But the Acadians had kept a low profile after the Deportation in case the British decided to repeat history. Living quietly and privately had become an old habit.

Annie led her to a table in the corner. The handful of musicians on the platform were warming up their fiddles and banjos; groups of people milled in and out of the kitchen area, mixing drinks, laughing and talking. Someone panted a few times into the microphone; catcalls and whistles rose from the crowd.

Annie smiled and nodded to people, her green eyes shining. Everyone knew Annie, it seemed. Their eyes went from Annie to her, examining the new person.

"Did you tell your husband where we were going?" Annie whispered, her face full of mischief.

"Why shouldn't I?" Claire answered evasively. She had told Annie and the other teachers that her husband was in poor health. That's how she explained her lack of social life. Annie didn't have to know everything.

"What did he say?" Annie's pixie face leaned into hers.

"He said...he said I looked nice," Claire replied. Annie

laughed conspiratorially.

Annie's husband had died in an accident at the shipyards six years before. There were no children, so she did what she pleased, whenever she pleased. Though Claire liked Annie, she didn't completely trust her. Why was she laughing like that? She had come to have a little fun, as Annie had suggested. Just to see what it was like, that was all, and to get some exercise. Dancing was good exercise.

When Jim Ryan and his Islanders started playing, the lights went down and people flooded onto the dance floor. The throb of fiddles, the smell of cigarettes and perfume filled the room, and Claire felt her senses sharpen, greedy for it all.

The dancers swirled around, bumped into each other, laughed and moved on. They were a jolly group, these Newfoundlanders, no doubt about it. They enjoyed life. They were a lot like the Acadians that way, Claire thought. There was always laughter and good spirits wherever the Acadians were.

"Who's that good-lookin' woman you got with you tonight, Annie?" she heard someone ask.

Claire turned toward the voice. She saw dimples, curly brown hair, wide brown eyes moving over her face.

"Claire, meet Joe," Annie said, winking.

"Do you suppose that good-lookin' woman might want to have a dance with me?" He spoke to Annie, but kept his eyes on Claire. His voice had the same looping Newfoundland lilt that Annie's did, a sound she'd come to associate with merriment, with good times.

Claire felt herself blushing as she smiled her consent. When she got up to follow him to the dance floor, Annie caught her arm. "Watch him," she whispered. "He's a good dancer and full of big talk, but he's married."

So what did that matter? Claire thought, feeling Joe's arm slip around her waist. She wasn't looking for a husband, just companionship—to be with someone her own age, someone who knew how to laugh instead of complain.

"You're the best thing I've seen here in months," Joe said, pulling her close.

Claire felt a shiver of pleasure. It was like being in a movie. She smelled his warm, masculine smell, felt his hand pressing against the small of her back. He was a good dancer, no doubt about it, she thought, feeling herself gliding along like a skater. The fiddles teased and taunted, the air thickened with smoke and the smell of bodies, alcohol and perfume. Something inside her broke free, floated upward.

Charles heard the sound of feet, several pairs, coming up the front steps. A loud knock came from the door. Since no-one else was home, he turned off the record player and padded over in his stockinged feet. André and Claude stood before him, their faces stiff with fear. Two men in uniforms stood by them. Red lights flashed at the curb in front of the house.

"Do these boys live here?"

"Yes, they're my sons."

"We picked them up around the corner," the taller policeman said. "We found these." He held out two packets of Black Cats and a handful of cherry bombs.

Charles stared at the policemen numbly. He should have known this would happen sooner or later.

The policeman said, "A woman down the street complained that some boys threw a bunch of firecrackers into her living-room. We took your boys by her house to see if they were the culprits. Lucky for them they weren't."

There was a kind of practiced menace in the policeman's tone. He'd dealt with boys, it said, and knew their tricks. Charles thought of all the times he had called the police himself because of thieves. Now here were his own boys, brought home in a police car like juvenile delinquents.

"You know, of course," the policeman continued, looking at him pointedly, "that firecrackers are illegal in this city?"

"I've told them over and over..." Charles began, then stopped. What was the use? The young were like that. You couldn't tell them anything. They played with fire until they got burned.

The other policeman gave him a sympathetic look, one that said he was a family man himself and understood how it was.

"You may want to keep a closer eye on them in the future," he said softly.

Charles thanked them, grateful that nothing more would come of it. He watched the two men go down the front steps. With the moon so full, it was almost as bright as day. How stupid of the boys to try something on a night like this.

He turned to face his sons. They had shrunk into themselves, refusing to meet his eyes. André's thin arms hung by his side. He had shot up this past summer and looked older than his fourteen years. Claude, his face and neck smudged with dirt, stared at the floor. They both smelled musty, as if they had been crawling around under someone's porch. They were expecting his rage, and by rights he should rage at them. Somehow, though, he just couldn't muster it.

"I hope you learned a lesson from this," he said, and sent them to bed.

15: Mud Time

"Dad said he'd give his permission," Annette was saying. Her eyes were averted. "And we've already talked to Father O'Connor about it. He said it would be better if you would give your permission, too, though it isn't really necessary. I'll be eighteen by then and legally an adult. But he said it's always better when both parents give their blessing, so I'm asking you again."

Claire watched Annette's face. Annette had waited until the others were occupied in front of the television before seeking her out.

"So, you've made up your mind," Claire said. It wasn't exactly a surprise, but the certainty of it made her sad. "I suppose you've already planned your guest list, too." She could hear the sarcasm in her tone, yet couldn't help herself.

Annette pursed her lips. "We've listed 82 so far; Emile has a lot of relatives. We're going to have the reception at the Lord Nelson."

Claire felt her mouth drop open. The Lord Nelson was an elegant, expensive hotel. Girls from the South End had their debutante balls there.

"Don't worry, you won't have to pay for anything," Annette said coldly. "I have some money saved up and Emile said he'd pay for the rest."

"That's not what I meant, Annette." Oh Lord, she thought. Would they quarrel for the rest of their lives?

"Your father has a lot of debts," she said in a softer voice. "But we'll contribute what we can."

"Are you giving us your blessing, then?"

Claire didn't answer for a moment, watching Annette's pale, stiff face. She felt chastened in the presence of such steely determination.

"I really hoped you would wait a few years, so you could find out who you were before you got married. But then, I suppose that in itself is no guarantee of a good marriage. I was 27..." *and look what I got myself into*, she almost said, but caught herself. "At least Emile is practical," she continued. "He works hard and seems to know how to manage money. That's important in a marriage. Much more important than you think. And though he's older than you are, I guess eleven years isn't all that bad. When you're 40, he'll be 51. Your father was 50 when I married him." She stopped for a moment and thought about herself and Charles. He was 69 now, centuries older than she, it seemed.

Annette was watching her expectantly, her hands folded together, as if in prayer.

Claire sighed. "Okay, Annette, I give you my blessing. In the sense that I wish you happiness, wish you a good marriage."

"Thank you, Mom," Annette said in a small voice and hugged her quickly. Annette had not hugged her in a long time.

After Annette left the kitchen, Claire stood at the counter remembering. Almost nineteen years ago, she and Charles had joined their lives together in the little church where she had been baptized and received her first Holy Communion. She, too, had paid for her own wedding. Her mother, who by then lived with Louie and his wife, was not in a position to help.

In a rush, images from that day came back to her: Louie and

Hebert looking clumsy and uncomfortable, their rough, farmers' hands dangling below the sleeves of their suits; Isabel in her new cold wave, her hair angling away from her face in little bent wires. Everything had felt dewy, veiled in mist— her pale silk wedding dress, the red rose in Charles' lapel. People told them they made a beautiful couple, and it seemed that way, with Charles so tall and slim, and she, feeling like a songbird beside him. On their wedding night, he had recited a poem he had written for her.

Claire felt a heaviness gather in her chest. Where had that person gone? Through the living-room doorway she could see Charles, crumpled in his chair in front of the television, his face thick and passive with watching. That was not the man she had married. That man was an impostor.

She went to the window and looked out over the backyards. A new snow had fallen and hung in soft cottony mounds on the roof tops, the picket fences, Mrs. Smith's lilac bush. Though the sun had set hours ago, the streetlights reflected off the snow making it seem almost as light as day. Maybe things would be better for Annette. Perhaps Emile would turn out to be as he seemed.

But then, maybe not. So many men were impostors. Joe, at the Newfoundland Club, had seemed so nice the first few times she met him there. But he drank too much. And like a drunken hummingbird, he darted from one pretty face to another.

Claire leaned into the trolley window and looked out, hoping to find some small sign. She examined the borders of the yards they passed, and the sheltered areas around the edges of houses. Even a tiny green shoot would have been enough; a nub of yellow or purple would have sent her into raptures. But the patches of earth not covered by old snow still looked shrivelled and hard. Spindly icicles hung from the edges of roofs half-heartedly, like bits of tinsel on a discarded Christmas tree.

Some Marches were full of the promise of spring, with winds that smelled damp and earthy, like a new garden. "Mud time," people called it, those first few weeks in late March or early April when the earth thawed and the ground became a squishy brown mass. Everyone complained, but nobody really minded: mud time meant that spring was finally on its way.

But so far, even mud time was nowhere in sight. Everything— the pot-holed streets, the subdued houses, the boney-fingered trees—looked worn-down, as if they could not endure another moment of winter. She studied the sky, a leaden, sullen grey; she couldn't remember the last time she had seen the sun. As they crossed the bridge, the harbour water lapped against itself like a wounded animal.

Even her students, usually so irrepressible, seemed heavy and dull these days. So today she had told them about pussy willows, how they signalled the coming of spring as surely as mud time did. Though it was still a few weeks early, she encouraged them to be on the lookout for the little furry buds. She would give a prize, she said, to the first one to bring in pussy willows. Twenty-three pairs of eyes looked up, and the classroom suddenly became alive. Colin and Joey and Annabel eagerly assured her that they would be the ones to win, and Gerald wondered in a loud voice what the prize would be. Remembering their excited faces made her smile.

A big pot of vegetable soup—that's what she would make for supper, she decided as she came in. And maybe some tea biscuits. It was early still, only 2.45 PM. Thank heaven she taught morning Primary now. After planning the next days's lessons, she could leave and be home in time to prepare a decent supper.

Dirty dishes from both breakfast and noon were neatly stacked in the sink, and someone had wiped the counter and table. Annette seldom came home at noon anymore, preferring to eat at work and save the trolley fare. Nicole must have come home today; it wouldn't occur to Charles and the boys to tidy up.

As Claire filled the sink with hot soapy water she heard someone knocking at the front door. She dried her hands on her apron and pushed her hair out of her face.

A man in a brown uniform and sheriff's badge stood there.

"Are you Mrs. LeBlanc?" he asked.

"Yes," she said, feeling a small tremor of fear run through her. She looked past him to the car idling by the fire hydrant, half expecting to see André and Claude in the back seat. They had sworn off firecrackers since the episode last fall, but you never knew. The car, however, was empty.

"I have a letter for Mr. and Mrs. Charles LeBlanc," the man said gravely. "You have ten days to respond." He touched the brim of his hat, turned, and went down the steps.

Claire tore open the letter. As she read, she felt the blood drain from her face. The floor undulated beneath her feet, and she clung to the doorjam as if she were drowning.

Nicole woke to the sound of crying. The clock on her desk read 1.10 AM. She lay in bed for a while listening. The house was cold; at night they kept the furnace low to save on oil. Sure enough, those were muffled sobs. Could it be Annette? Had something happened between her and Emile?

Nicole stuck a bare foot tentatively out from under the covers. Yikes, it was cold. She sloughed into her slippers, pulled on her robe and tiptoed into the hall. She listened by Annette's partly open door. Nothing. The sounds were coming from her mother's room. Come to think of it, her mother had been queer and silent at suppertime. Her door was closed, but a thin border of light came from underneath. Nicole tapped lightly and entered.

"Mom, I heard you. Is something wrong?" Her mother, wrapped in a quilt, lay across the dishevelled bed. An assortment of letters and papers fanned out around her. When she saw Nicole she sat up and tried to compose herself.

"It's nothing dear, really. I couldn't sleep and... I'm sorry I woke you." Her mouth was twisted and purplish, and without her makeup she looked small and vulnerable.

"Is it something one of us did?" Nicole asked, suddenly afraid.

"No," her mother said. "You children are more precious to me than anything in the world." She threw her arms around Nicole and wept onto her neck until Nicole felt like crying too. Then she sat up and dabbed at her swollen nose with a

Kleenex. "I just don't know what to do, Nicole. I shouldn't tell you about this, but I have no-one to turn to. Oh your father! How could he do this to us!" She rummaged among the papers on the bed and handed one to Nicole. Nicole stared at the black type, the official-looking words, the seal on the bottom.

"They want to take our house and throw us out into the street," her mother said. "The sheriff came to our door with that letter this afternoon. Can you imagine?"

"Your father's debts," she continued. "He owes so much money! They warned him over and over, but he didn't even answer their letters. Now they want their money, even if it means taking our house."

Nicole felt something in the bottom of her stomach lurch. She had lived in this house all her life. What would happen to them? Where would they go? She pictured all their furniture, her white wrought-iron bed, her maple desk, piled on the sidewalk, while strangers walked into their house, closed the door and locked them out.

"Your father says there's nothing he can do, that he has no money," her mother said. "He says he'll try to sell the business and use that money to pay off the bills, but who would want to buy it? There's nothing left of it!" Her voice came in breathy spurts and she rocked as she spoke. "I didn't want you to know, Nicole. I don't want any of you to have to worry about this."

Nicole had never seen her mother like this before. A slow terror gripped her. Would they have to camp out in someone's backyard, like she'd done some summer nights when she was a child? She imagined the neighbourhood dogs, sniffing at them while they slept. Where would she keep her books, her dresses?

"We can't let them take our house, Mom," she said in a trembling voice. "We have to do something."

"I've been trying to figure out what to do," her mother said. "These are the bills." She gestured toward the papers on the bed. Nicole recognized the familiar letterheads of McCormick, Ganong, Cadbury. A Credit Union passbook lay open beside them.

"I hardly earn enough to pay for the mortgage and the food. There's the oil and clothing and electricity and bus fare... I've been adding it up over and over. There just isn't enough for his bills too."

Nicole thought of the $43.00 hidden at the bottom of her blue jewellery box. It seemed like so little, suddenly. She looked at her mother, at the lines around her eyes she hadn't noticed before. Beyond her, under the window, stood her mother's cedar hope chest. Her mother had had it since she was a girl.

"Maybe...," Nicole said, choking out the words, "Maybe I could quit school and get a job at Zeller's, like Annette."

Claire felt herself jolted, as if she'd been slapped. She became very still for a moment. "No, Nicole, you won't quit school," she found herself saying in a voice suddenly calm. "This is not your responsibility." She put her arms around Nicole and held her.

"But what'll we do, Mom?"

"I have an idea," Claire said, trying hard to think of one as she went along. "Maybe I can offer to pay a little at a time; maybe they'll be satisfied with that. Yes, and then maybe while they're distracted, I can get the house put in my name. That way we'd be safe. They couldn't take the house for your father's debts if the house were in my name."

"Do you really think that would work?" "Yes," she said. The more she thought about it, the more she thought it might.

"Besides, your father might find a buyer for the business. You never know. But you mustn't worry about it Nicole. I promise you things will be all right. I'll call them tomorrow, those candy companies. But don't tell Annette or the boys about all this. It's not good for them to know."

Nicole hugged her mother again and returned to bed. She lay there for a long time, thinking of her mother in the room down the hall crying, of her father downstairs sleeping.

When she fell asleep, she dreamed she came home from school and found the doors to the house wide open. It was snowing, and huge gusts were blowing in through the open doors, forming drifts as far in as the sofa. Her father's truck stood outside by the basement doors, but nobody was home. Frantic, she grabbbed the broom and began sweeping out the snow, but the harder she swept, the harder the wind blew. Sheets of snow swirled round and round her. She could no longer see, but still she kept sweeping.

The next day when Nicole came home from school she found her father in his chair, reading.

"Didn't you go out today?" she asked.

"My back hurt so much I..."

He doesn't care, she thought. *He doesn't even care that we could lose our house.*

Claire didn't want the children to hear, so she shut the door behind her. Charles sat on the edge of the bed taking off his shoes, his breath heavy and raspy with the effort. Almost five years had passed since they had been alone together in this room with the door shut. Occasionally she still sat at the vanity with the big round mirror when she put on her makeup, but underneath the scent of her powder and cosmetics, she could smell a creeping old man's smell. His bladder had begun to weaken; on Saturdays his longjohns smelled of urine.

"They told me that as long as we pay something every month they'd leave us alone," she told him. "I offered them $10.00. It's all I can spare but they said they'd take it for now."

Charles nodded.

Claire felt anger leap up inside of her. He couldn't even say he was sorry. Instead, he just sat there, saying nothing, oblivious to what she had been through. She had called the candy company that was bringing suit, told them that her husband was ill, that he could no longer handle his affairs, that they were putting the business up for sale. They had four children at home, she'd said. She was doing the best she could on a teacher's salary; she'd pay a little at a time as she could. She had appealed to their sense of decency, their compassion. She had humiliated herself, made herself sound helpless, defenseless. She had even cried a little, when all along she had wanted to rage at them—how dare they try to take her home.

But it meant nothing to him. It was the same old story repeating itself again and again, starting with that first accident, when she had had to fend for herself and the children. It seemed to her now that he was a great burden, a weight set around her neck like some hideous necklace.

"What do you plan to do about the other debts you owe?" she asked. Several other companies, she had discovered, were threatening to file judgments against them.

"When I sell the business there should be enough money to pay them off," he said. "I'm going to put an ad in the paper this weekend."

"See that you do," she said.

The look Claire gave Charles as she left the room pierced him. Couldn't she see that he had done the best he could? It wasn't his fault that his health had gotten so bad he couldn't keep up anymore. Well, fine. If she wanted to be angry with him, let her be. He'd sell the business, then she'd see. Tomorrow, first thing, he'd make a list of all his regular customers. His inventory was low, but the new buyer could have what remained. He could sell the truck separately, perhaps. It was still in pretty good shape and might bring in a few extra dollars. He would talk to Emile, too. Maybe Emile had some Lebanese friend looking for a start in life. It would make a fine business for a young man with energy and drive.

He lay back on the bed, folded his arms behind his head and stretched out his legs. A curious relief spread through him. He wouldn't have to go in the truck anymore. He wouldn't have to carry those heavy boxes and fret over supplies and thieves. All those worries that had inhabited his body for years like so many more aches and pains, now seemed to rise up out of him, flutter in the air, and disappear like vapour.

Nicole watched her father lift the fork to his mouth. Everything about him irritated her now, but mealtimes were the worst. The way his mouth moved when the dish of potatoes or the bowl of gravy came his way. Her mother noticed it too, and reminded him that there were five other people at the table who needed to eat as well. He responded with a kind of snarling noise, like an animal. "Mom is so mean to Dad these days," Annette remarked later. "Did you hear what she said to him at supper?"

"It's because he won't work anymore."

"He's 69," Annette said. "He's old and tired and his body hurts. He just can't do it anymore."

You don't know what he's done, Nicole thought. *You don't know.*

In early April it began raining, and the earth became a sea of mud. Every day it rained, sometimes in sudden hard bursts, sometimes in a steady cold drizzle. Claire watched the harbour waters as she rode the bus over the Halifax-Dartmouth bridge. The water and sky were the same grey as the girders; grey trawlers lurked below, hugging grey wharfs. She imagined, for a moment, what it would be like to fall into that grey water. Two hundred years ago a Micmac Indian had put a curse on any bridge that would connect Halifax and Dartmouth. Two bridges had collapsed. A Micmac Chieftain had lifted the curse just before this bridge opened, but many people were still afraid to cross it.

Sometimes it seemed that a curse had been placed on her life, too. In the three weeks since Charles had started advertizing in the *Chronicle Herald* there had been only two calls. Neither had led to anything. How would they live?

She stopped at the store to pick up bread and a pound of hamburger. Holding her umbrella against the relentless rain, she walked the two blocks home. April showers bring May flowers, she told her pupils, but it seemed as if nothing beautiful could ever come from this mess.

Her boots made squishing noises and her feet felt cold. She and the children placed their boots upside down over the furnace vents every night, but in the morning, the boots still felt clammy inside. They had tried putting them in the oven to dry, but after a few minutes the whole house smelled of rubber. When she got home she found Charles sitting on a stool at the kitchen counter peeling vegetables.

"I thought I would get these started for you," he said.

She looked at the neat pile of peeled potatoes and carrots. He had washed the noon dishes, too, and put them away.

"Thank you," she said. Even her anger against him had turned to a dull grey.

One afternoon a man called in response to the ad. He wasn't

135

interested in the business, he said, but he could use a good truck. Charles followed the man around while he looked at it.

"The tires look a bit worn, do you suppose they have much life left in them?"

"Oh they'll get you through till next fall, anyway," Charles answered. "I have chains for them, too, if you want them; I won't be needing them." If he could sell the truck, there would be a little cash to tide them over.

"It's rusted pretty bad around the fenders here."

"It's been through a lot of winters; you can't help that. But it runs well. It's never let me down."

The man kept glancing at him, as if he were searching for something.

"You sound right familiar," the man said, finally. "Did you ever work over at Veteran's Affairs?"

"Why, yes, I did," Charles said. "For a few years during and after the second war."

The man's face opened into a smile and he put out his hand.

"You probably don't remember, but you found me a job after I come back from over there. I've been working at the Abattoir for fifteen years now."

There had been so many men, most of them young, their eyes still haunted by what they had seen. He didn't remember this one, but he took the man's hand and smiled back. They talked for a while longer, then the man put some bills into Charles' hand and drove off with the truck. They hadn't even haggled over the price.

Nicole heard someone calling her over. Mrs. Smith stood at her front door, waving. "Is the Monsieur sick?" she asked. "I don't see his truck going by anymore. I hope he's not sick again." Mrs. Smith's face was yellow and the smell of kitchen grease drifted out from over her shoulder. Last night they had heard Mr. Smith yelling in the alleyway again, even though it wasn't payday. "No, he's not," Nicole said carefully, avoiding Mrs. Smith's eyes. "He sold the truck. He wants to sell the business and retire. That's why he's home all the time now."

"Oh, I see," Mrs Smith said, relieved, the corners of her mouth fluttering downward. "Well, that's good. Your poor father has worked hard his whole life. He deserves some rest now. He's a good man, your father."

Down the street three little girls were playing jumprope in spite of the drizzle. One of them broke away from the others and yelled: "You lie!"

"You're the liar!" the other two called back. "Liar, liar, pants on fire, hanging on the telephone wire!"

"I talked to everyone I know about your husband's business," Emile told Claire. "But no-one's interested. Not many stores carry penny candy anymore." He looked down. "I told Mr. LeBlanc I'd buy the chips he has left—I can always sell those. But the penny candy..." He shook his head.

Claire studied his face. He didn't know about the sheriff and the threat to the house; Charles wouldn't have told him and Nicole could keep secrets.

"Thank you, Emile," Claire said. "I appreciate your efforts."

"I wish there was more I could do, Mrs. LeBlanc."

There was no hint of teasing and bantering in his voice anymore. He was just Emile, and he was trying to help them.

"Call me Claire," Claire said, touching his arm. "After all, you're almost part of the family."

Toward the end of April Gerald brought in a whole armload of pussywillows and bragged to the class that he and his father had seen a bear while they were out in the woods.

"I think it's a bit early for bears," Claire told him. "They're still hibernating."

"Well, he was rubbing his eyes and looked sleepy," Gerald said, his own eyes big. She made up a bag of pennycandy as the prize. They might as well use it for something.

16: Sodom and Gomorrah

Nicole had never seen so many Lebanese all at once. All those square jaws and fierce bright eyes, all that thick dark hair, those red mouths with shadowy upper lips. Now, standing between Annette and her mother in the receiving line, she could study them more closely.

Someone grabbed her by the waist and kissed her on the mouth. "I'm Antoon," he said. "A cousin of the groom and official photographer." He had taken pictures of them at the church, though he had not said he was Emile's cousin.

"I remember you," she said, not knowing what else to say to that big, aggressive smile. But he was moving on, and had grabbed her mother and was kissing her. "Ah, the mother of the bride, as beautiful as the bride herself," he said.

Later, when it seemed that she had been kissed and patted by the whole Lebanese population of Halifax, Nicole went up to the suite Emile had rented for all of them to use as a changing area. She squinted at herself in the mirror and adjusted a few pins in her french roll.

"Admiring yourself again, are you?" André said as he and Claude came in from the bedroom. They were wearing jackets and ties, the first they'd ever owned. Claire had ordered them from the Simpson's catalogue and was paying for them in installments. The boys looked sweaty and rumpled; they'd been up to something.

"What were you guys doing in there?" she asked, giving them a sharp look. "Annette and Emile's stuff is in there."

They giggled and jostled each other. "Listen, you're allowed to play tricks on people when they get married," André said. "We'll tell you if you promise not to tell."

They led her into the bedroom where Annette's and Emile's suitcases lay on the bed, and opened Annette's. Her clothes were all folded neatly inside. Claude carefully lifted the pale peach chiffon nightdress with cream-coloured lace Annette had bought for her wedding night, and on the robe underneath lay a huge furry black spider. Nicole gasped. The boys hooted with laughter.

"It's not real," Claude said, "but she won't know that for a while. We put one inside a shoe, too, and one in her jewellery box. There's also a big plastic cockroach in there, but we won't tell you where." They grinned knowingly. Nicole pictured them fingering Annette's bras and panties and felt herself flush. She thought of her own rumpled underwear at home in her drawers.

"That's terrible!" she said. "I should tell."

"C'mon, it isn't going to hurt anything," André said. "Don't be a spoilsport."

She gave them a disgusted look and went back downstairs.

Lines had begun forming by the food table. Emile's mother and sisters and several other female relatives had been cooking for days. Annette told her, "I'm going to learn how to cook all that stuff. It's so good. Wait till you try it." The tables were laden with meat pastries, glossy brown whole chickens, stuffed vine leaves, lamb mixed with grain, parsley salads, dips covered with oil, platters of small stuffed eggplant, bowls of yogurt. The whole table smelled of garlic and mint and roasted meats.

She put a little of everything on her plate, then looked around for a place to sit. Everything looked festive—white tablecloths, pink napkins and candles, tiny foil cups with pink and white Jorden almonds by each place.

Annette, holding up the long train of her dress, was looking out over the crowd as if she couldn't quite believe all this was for her. She saw Nicole and waved for her to come over. "Go sit with Dad, will you. He's over there by himself."

Nicole felt her neck stiffen. "Where's Mom?"

"She's around somewhere. Dad shouldn't have to sit by himself."

"Okay," Nicole said. She'd do it for Annette.

Her father, sitting at one of the big round tables, was already eating. Nicole sat a few spaces away. "Your sister made a good match," he said.

"Yes," she said, occupying herself with her food. In his good grey suit, he looked different from the way he looked at home, sitting around in his old workpants and longjohns. He leaned toward her, as if he wanted to say something else, something private and nice, just to her. "This stuff is really good," she said loudly. "Did you try these pastries? They have pine nuts in them. Annette said she was going to learn how to make them."

André and Claude appeared at the table, each with a plate.

"That stuff looks weird," André said.

"Too bad they don't have any bread and molasses," Nicole said.

"Very funny."

Now that the boys were here, she could leave. "I'm going to walk around a little," she announced.

She found her mother and Antoon standing by the food table.

"Nicole," her mother said, grabbing her hand. "You've met Antoon, haven't you?"

"Yes," Nicole said, nodding at him.

"Antoon speaks the most beautiful French. Did you know that French is the cultural language of Lebanon?"

"No, I didn't," she said. Her mother's cheeks were bright pink, as if she had put on too much rouge.

"Many Lebanese speak it," her mother continued. "Emile speaks it a little, though he never told us he did. Imagine that! Isn't that wonderful?"

Her mother kept holding her hand as if she wanted to keep her there, but instead of looking at Nicole she looked at Antoon. It was hard to tell how old he was—older than Emile, but younger than her mother. He was leaning over her, smiling at her with his big teeth.

"I'm going to get something to drink," Nicole said, pulling her hand away. "I think they have some pop over there."

A band was forming at one end of the room. Annette had told her there would be dancing. Everywhere, people were laughing, talking loudly, eating.

Her father had gotten himself another plate of food. Annette was standing by him, holding her train in the crook of her arm, touching his shoulder with her hand. He was smiling at her, as an ordinary father would. *Annette doesn't know*, she reminded herself. *Annette doesn't know what he's done.*

On the other side of the room a long line of people began dancing to Arabic music. A man holding a white handkerchief led the dancers in a circle while they stamped their feet and kicked out their legs. Her mother and Antoon were among them, Antoon holding her mother by the waist, her mother holding the waist of the man in front of her. Her mother's face was flushed, her head thrown back in hot laughter.

She could join them, she thought. She could go over, and

someone would grab her, make room for her in the line. And she would dance and laugh like all the others. But somehow she couldn't move. She leaned against the wall and watched them. It was as if the whole room and everyone in it were part of an elaborate, happy dream. She was the only one who knew what was real.

Sometimes she imagined him dead. What would their lives be like? Her mother would be free to go out with anyone she wanted to without pretending. The house would smell better. She made a mental list, then hated herself. *He is my father.*

She didn't want him talking to her, noticing her. When he did he said old-man things, like complaining about the length of her skirt. She had saved up a long time for this white pleated skort with attached bloomers, perfect for her job at the playground. No doubt he'd have some comment to make. She passed him in his chair; though it was summer, he wore thick grey wool socks with red heels and toes.

"You're not wearing that outside, I hope," he said, peering at her over his book. He was always reading books now, religious books by Fulton J. Sheen, Thomas Aquinas, Saint Augustine. That's all he did.

"What's wrong with it?" she asked, her voice like ice.

"It's immodest," he said, his voice rising. "That's what's wrong with it. Anyone can see the seat of your pants if they look."

"The pants are part of it," she said, pulling up the skirt and wiggling her bloomered behind at him. "They're just shorts with a little skirt over them." She knew she was taunting him, didn't care.

"By God, you're not going outside with those on," he yelled, struggling to get up from the chair, his face chalky red.

"Try and stop me," she said, slamming the door behind her.

She ran the first block up toward Connaught Avenue, flushed with triumph. After that she slowed down; she didn't want to arrive at her job at the playground out of breath or looking too eager. She walked the mile each way to save carfare; every dime she saved went toward her secret fund, her get-away-from-here fund. A breeze rustled around her bare

141

legs and her skort flared. Summer had not settled in yet, and her legs felt cool and exposed. Across the street a man and woman were watching her. What if they thought she really was wearing a very short skirt, and that the bloomers really were her underpants? She let her arms hang limp by her sides, so she could hold down the edges of her skort. Maybe she should have gotten the navy blue ones instead, so it would be clear that the skirt and bloomers were a set.

Sometimes at night she heard her mother crying. She'd lie awake in her own bed, rigid with listening. She had stopped going into her mother's room at night; she couldn't stand seeing her that way. Her mother had put the house in her name, but now the creditors threatened to take the furniture. Her mother showed her the letters. "Don't tell anyone," she said. Her mother answered all the letters, sending a few dollars each time.

Meanwhile, her father sat in his chair like a lump of dough. He'd stopped trying to sell the business. No-one wanted it, he explained, shrugging his shoulders. *You could at least keep trying*, she yelled at him inside. All summer André and Claude opened the remaining boxes of candy without even asking. No-one seemed to care that they were gradually eating it all or giving it away to their friends.

One day in September Claude came running home with dark red blood streaming from his nose, all the way down his shirt to his waist.

"He fell out of the MacDonald's tree and landed on the garage roof, face first," André told them, breathless.

No-one asked what they were doing there, Nicole noticed. They were always up to something, those boys. She held a cold wet washrag to his nose while her mother called the neighbours to see if anyone could take them to the Infirmary.

Later, her father said: "You'd make a good nurse," and smiled at her softly. "I don't plan to be a nurse," she told him coldly.

She didn't know what she wanted to be yet, but it wasn't that. And it wasn't any of his business. What did he know, anyway? She'd get a good job, whatever it was. She'd make as much money as a man. And when she did, she'd pay off all the candy companies so they'd leave her mother alone. Then she'd buy her mother some nice things.

But first she had to go to college.

Mother Connolly said: "Maryville College in the States has a good scholarship. You could try for that. They offer it every year to a foreign student from a Sacred Heart School. The exams are in March. Of course, it's a long way from home. The Mount and Dal are closer, but their scholarships are only partial. Maryville offers room and board as well as full tuition."

Nicole went to the library and took a World Atlas off the shelf. She turned to New York state, then to Long Island, where Maryville was. A lot of other girls would be competing. Convent girls from Latin America, from Africa, from Europe. She traced the borders of continents with her finger.

She began getting up at 6.30 AM. She learned how to wake her-self, so that when her father called from the foot of the stairs she had already been studying her Latin for half an hour. She hurried through breakfast, and if she got a seat on the bus, went over her Algebra homework. If she had to stand, she recited poems she memorized for English. She brought a sandwich everyday now, and a jelly jar of milk, and ate in the cloakroom, so she could get in another hour of study—time that would otherwise be wasted. She stayed in the study hall with the boarding students until 5.00 PM when they were called to supper and she had to go home. After supper, she studied upstairs in her room until ten. When it got cold, she wrapped a blanket around herself and wore her gloves. There was so much to learn.

"God, you're queer these days," Meredith said to her. "You always have your nose in a book. What's the matter with you?"

"Nothing. I'm just doing my homework."

"Well, I do my homework, too, but Lord, there are other things, you know."

But there was nothing else. Everything else was a black hole.

She had to make the highest marks in everything. That way she'd know she was getting somewhere. That way, when she took the exams in March, she'd know she had done the best she could.

She studied her French. Mother McGuire had all the girls try out for a French contest. They made tapes of everyone reading a certain passage. It was for the Canada Prize. Since that first French class when Mother McGuire had winced at her "country French," Nicole had been careful about how she said things. She had not volunteered a word in class for months after that. But now she was very good at Parisian pronunciation. She could trill her Rs like a real French girl.

Every now and then, when her mother heard her practising, she said: "Acadian French is not bad French, Nicole. It's just different, the way Canadian English is different from British English." But Nicole didn't care. If the nuns said to say "ici" instead of "icit," then that's what it would be. The nuns at Maryville would speak like the Parisians, not the Acadians.

Sometimes she took a few hours off on a Saturday afternoon to visit Annette. Six months married and she was five months pregnant. She and Emile lived in two rooms. Three roomers lived upstairs, and two in the room that was supposed to be the living-room, but was walled off. Annette and Emile slept in the room that had once been the dining-room; a curtain separated it from the large kitchen. They were paying off the mortgage with the rent money.

"It's only for a few more months," Annette explained. "When the baby is born we'll take back the room down here and only have roomers upstairs."

Annette was sitting by the window on a low cot that served as a sofa. They were both waiting for things, she and Annette. Things that would happen in May.

"What's it like to be pregnant?"

"It's different," Annette said. "It's nice, now that I don't throw up anymore."

"I don't think I'll ever have babies," Nicole said.

"Yes you will. Everyone does."

Christmas Eve came. Her mother made a rabbit pie to eat after midnight mass like she always did. But this time she said, "There's going to be a French mass in Dartmouth. There are a lot of Acadians and French from Quebec in Shannon Park. They don't want to forget their culture. Things are changing now." She and her mother sang Minuit Chretien and heard a French sermon. Her father and brothers waited until morning and went to Saint Catherine's.

On New Year's Eve, her mother put on a new black dress with silver threads in it. "I'm meeting some friends," she told Nicole. She put her heavy brown coat on over her glittering dress and slipped out. Nicole knew she was meeting Antoon. She recognized his voice on the phone when he asked for her mother. He had been calling since summer.

Nicole stayed up until midnight reading, a quilt wrapped around her. When she heard the bells pealing in the New Year, she went to the window. The streets were empty. Her father and the boys had gone to bed long before, so the house was dark. Most of the other houses were dark, too, except for the occasional porchlight. She felt a curious sensation staring at the quiet houses, the starry sky. She was part of it and not part of it. Somewhere, in some warm place, her mother was laughing with Antoon.

March. Only a few weeks left before the exams. Her body felt like a wire. The more she studied, the more she saw how much there was to learn.

The night before the exams, her mother made fried smelts and baked apples. "Have a good dinner, then go to bed early," she told Nicole. "The best preparation now is a good night's rest." Her mother seemed almost as nervous as she was, pacing around the kitchen.

"If I win, I'll only need money for books and clothes and to come home at Christmas. I could get a waitressing job somewhere in the summers to pay for all that." She had made herself not talk about it these past few months. Now she couldn't stop talking about it.

Her father hadn't said much. He wasn't eating and seemed to be thinking about something.

"I'm not sure all this is a good idea, Nicole," he said finally.

"What's not a good idea?"

"New York is not a place for a young girl by herself."

"Dad, I'd be living in a dorm." She said, "Sure I'd want to

go into the city now and then—who wouldn't? Don't worry, I'd be careful."

"I lived in New York for a few years with my brother, Claude." She knew vaguely that he had lived in the States, but she had never heard the details. None of it had anything to do with her, anyway.

"We saw all kinds of things there. It's not a place for a young girl by herself. It's like Sodom and Gomorrah."

André and Claude stopped eating to listen. Their father never talked about his life before them.

"Sodom and Gomorrah," he said again, looking like an Old Testament prophet.

Nicole glared at him. He was trying to spoil things, to stand in her way. "I don't care what it's like," she said. "I'm going if I get the chance to, no matter what."

His colour was rising. She knew it made him boiling mad when she talked like this, but she couldn't help herself.

"You don't care," he said sputtering in rage. "You don't care. Well you'd care if I had you recalled at the border."

Nicole felt herself turn white with hatred. "If you ever did that, I'd run away. You'd never see me again, any of you."

"Look, nobody's going to have anybody recalled at the border," her mother said firmly. "Stop this, both of you!"

His mouth was still moving, his face bright red, but she no longer heard him. *He should be dead*, she thought. *We'd all be better off if he were dead.*

She kept studying. The exams were over but she couldn't make herself relax. It was as if studying even now could make her exam answers better. She felt she had done well, but maybe all the others had felt that way too. All those other Convent girls from all over the world, all wanting her prize.

In the second week of May, Annette had her baby. A boy. After the Baptism, there was a party at Annette and Emile's. Nicole went to help. All afternoon, the Lebanese came and went. The men drank arak mixed with water, the women sipped hot sugared tea in thin glasses. Emile's brother kept undoing the baby's diaper and cupping his hand around the baby's genitals to show some male relative. "Stop that," his wife said to him. "That's not your child." But Annette didn't seem to mind. She moved among them, making sure that everyone had a serving of the traditional rice pudding served at Lebanese christenings. She had made it herself. She cooked nothing but Lebanese food now; even the bread. Nicole thought: she has become one of them.

In a week she'd know. She propped herself up in bed to read. Through the partially open window, scents floated in, musky, warm-earth smells—the green smell of new leaves, the fresh, windy smell of sheets that had hung on a line all day. A crescent moon, sharp as a fingernail, shone in the sky. Her mother was out. Not with Antoon this time, but with someone else. Antoon had stopped calling.

Suddenly Nicole heard a shriek. She shut off her light and looked out the window. Doreen Smith was standing under Mrs. Holland's big maple tree crying while her sailor wrestled with something. She could barely see them; the tree with its great canopy was larger than all the others on the street and away from the streetlight. Doreen and her sailor often said goodnight there. The sailor threw something to the sidewalk, where it lay in a rumpled heap next to Doreen's feet. He looked up into the tree and shook his fist.

"Wait till I get you, you brats!" he shouted. Two boys dropped out of the branches and tore down the street, the sailor following in hot pursuit. Lord, was that André and Claude? In a little while, the sailor came back. He picked up the thing lying on the sidewalk then threw it back down in disgust. It looked like a scarecrow, and it was wearing one of her father's old flannel shirts.

Lights had come on in a few houses. The sailor, muttering low curses, led Doreen across the street to her house.

Though Nicole felt sorry for Doreen, she couldn't help but smile. She pictured her brothers hiding under some porch, Claude with his fat cheeks and rabbit teeth saying: Did you see the look on his face when we dropped it? André returning: When he looked up and saw us, I thought I'd pee in my pants—the two of them falling over each other laughing.

147

What would they think of next? A few weeks ago she'd seen Claude furtively studying a library book on explosives. Maybe she wouldn't be here to see, she thought. Thank God.

It was 11.10 PM. She got back under the covers and decided to sleep. She heard her father shuffle to the front door and open it. "Here puss, puss," he called. Her father hardly ever tried to talk to her anymore. After a while, she heard him padding back to his bedroom, and she fell asleep.

A shaft of moonlight came through the window, waking her. It looked like a silver rope, so she decided to climb it. Up and up into the sky she went, into the fresh, green-smelling, starry May night. Everything was so beautiful. She could almost touch the stars. She floated among them for a long time, weightless, free. Then it was time to go home, time to slide down the beam, slide back into her own warm bed. When she turned, however, the moonbeam-rope had disappeared. There was no way to get back. She stared at the little house below, at the soft yellow light coming from a few of its windows. The sky was darkening. It was getting cold. She had never seen her house from this angle before; it looked so snug, so peaceful. Her father appeared at the back door. "Here puss, puss," he called. "Dad!" she shouted. But he couldn't hear her. Her heart lurched with longing.

17: One Last Time

Nicole struggles the wheels of the stroller up over the curb. Her four-month-old son, wrapped in a blue snowsuit, bobs forward in the seat. She has not had an uninterrupted night's sleep in weeks, so this November morning she is very tired.

Seven years have passed. Nicole is now married to David, the older brother of a girl she met at Marysville. David has olive skin and long graceful limbs. He recently finished his PhD in History, and two months ago, they moved to this college town in Michigan where David is now teaching.

Nicole stares at the little blue mummy. What could be the matter with him that he would wake two or three times every night? Perhaps it is their new surroundings. She glances at the leafless trees, their naked, vulnerable limbs. Already winter has descended upon the town like a weight, the earth hardened like a fist. She looks at the faces passing. White plumes of breath float out of their mouths. None of the faces are familiar. None of the faces looks back.

She parks the stroller outside their duplex and carries the baby and his bag of things up the four steep steps to the side door. She takes off his snowsuit and puts him in the baby seat. Then she carries in the two bags of groceries and puts them on the counter while she takes off her own heavy coat, hat, scarf and boots. So much effort to do the simplest things! Barely noon, and already she is exhausted.

The baby is making noises; it is time to feed him. She prepares a bottle, noting the dirty ones soaking in the sink, the pile of laundry waiting in the basket. Every day is the same. Hours and hours of changing and holding and feeding and getting things ready. This child has taken over her life; there is nothing left.

After he finishes his bottle, she collapses with him on the sofa for a few minutes. He perches on her chest, trying to do pushups. His mouth opens in a gummy smile.

"Don't you think seven-thirty would be a much nicer time to get up in the morning than six?" she asks him, yawning. A blob of saliva oozes down from his mouth onto her neck. He chortles, as if she has told him a wonderful joke.

They hadn't planned on having a baby just yet, but had accepted the news cheerfully. And the pregnancy had been lovely, all those evenings curled with David on the sofa, the tranquil dreams spun around the coming of this child.... Who would have thought it would be so much work? That it would take so much time? Annette hadn't warned her. Annette with her three little ones. How on earth did she manage with *three*? If only Annette were around to show her how to do it. Or her mother, who had somehow, miraculously it seemed now, survived having four.

Her mother had come for a few days after the birth. Her mother, in a new burgundy suit with matching shoes, the grey in her hair carefully hidden. She seemed younger than the last time Nicole had seen her, as if the process of ageing had reversed and she were now spiralling down toward youth.

"Paul is a good Acadian name," she said, cooing over the baby. "He looks like the LeBlancs, too. Make sure you let him know that he's half Acadian and talk to him in French."

Her mother taught solely in French now. Trudeau had introduced mandatory bilingualism; her mother's school in Dartmouth offered total immersion French classes, and her mother was helping to design the curriculum.

While she, Nicole, was involved in total immersion motherhood, she thinks glumly. She had quit her accounting job toward the end of her pregnancy, and planned to start a home accounting service after they moved, when things got settled. But everything seemed easier, possible, before the baby, or "BB" as she has begun to refer to that time. She thinks of the neat files in her desk, the lists of businesses, potential clients—all untouched. Six weeks in this new town, and she has not yet found the energy even to settle in. Unopened boxes lurk in the corners of the house; uncurtained windows stare reproachfully.

She tries to imagine the time when she will no longer feel this way, when her energy will return, and she will be her old self. Surely it will happen. But at this moment, lying on the sofa, it is a time unimaginable. "How come you hardly ever look tired? Huh? How come?" she asks the fourteen-pound bundle wiggling on her chest. His eyelids begin to droop, but he rouses himself and reaches for her nose.

"It's beddy-bye time now anyway," she says getting up.

Every afternoon, the baby sleeps. At least he is consistent in that. She thinks of the two or three hours that lie ahead as a gift. A blessing. She arranges the blanket over his little back, over his raised, padded bottom. She aches to fall into her own bed, too, but she is afraid. Sometimes when she naps in the afternoon something strange happens. Her mind or spirit—she is not sure what to call it, this thing that holds consciousness—slips out of her body like a swimmer shedding her clothes by the side of a stream. It hovers in the air detached, but close to the body, as if, like the swimmer, it dares not swim too far from the shelter of the clothing resting on the bank. It should be a pleasant feeling, she thinks, that sudden unencumbered state. But there are noises: the windows rattle like bones, the cupboards in the kitchen creak like footsteps, the furnace bleats and moans like anger. The spirit, eyeless, naked, twitches nervously, like a candle flame. *Listen*, it tells the body. *Do you hear that?* But the body, sluggish and stubborn, sleeps on. Fear mounts, shrill and constant like a high-pitched siren. *You must wake up! Something terrible will happen!* Finally, mind and body snap together and she jolts awake trembling, her hair damp against her neck.

Only these last six weeks, only since the move, has this strange thing happened. She has not told David. She doesn't want to worry him, especially now, with his new job.

No, she won't try to sleep. Instead, she will prepare something special for dinner tonight, a surprise for David. They used to have such lovely dinners, BB. Or perhaps she will write to her mother, or unpack a few more boxes.

But her limbs feel thick and numb, and refuse to move. She sits on the sofa and looks out the living-room window. A mood is settling upon her, entering her like a vapour. It is the mood of another day, another time—five years earlier.

Her mother had summoned her from her summer waitressing job on Long Island. "Come right away," she had said, "if you want to see your father alive one last time." When Nicole arrived, what she found on the hospital bed was not the father she remembered, but a shrunken facsimile.

"Mr. LeBlanc, your daughter has come to see you," the nurse barked into a grey ear. "Your daughter from the States. She's come all this way."

Pale green tubes coiled into his arms and slithered into his nose like snakes. His mouth, without the plastic teeth, had collapsed inward and fell partly open.

"Mr. LeBlanc," the nurse urged again. "This is the daughter you've been asking after." The nurse was stout, with broad hips and a pink, Scottish face. "Can you open your eyes and say hello?"

It had all happened so quickly. Four months before, he had been his usual self, his heavy body moulding to the old easy chair with the broken springs, a pile of theology books on the floor beside him, growling at everyone, and stinking in those longjohns he changed once a week. In June he had gone for tests. "The usual complaints," her mother had written. "You know your father." Then suddenly, he had begun leaving—60 pounds of him had disappeared in two and a half months. All that remained was this thin, silent grey body she barely recognized.

Later that day Nicole visited the basement. It had once been her father's turf, and now that he was dying, she felt drawn there. Halfway down the stairs, she was met by the familiar smell of dampness and decay. It was worse than ever. There was junk everywhere—broken furniture, scraps of linoleum, empty jars and bags, outgrown and worn out clothing, parts from old cars that André and Claude had salvaged. Three overflowing garbage cans stood near the large wooden doors where her father used to drive in the truck.

Her father's old desk stood in its usual corner under the front window. Scattered papers and half-opened drawers gave it an interrupted look, as if someone working there had suddenly been called away. Now everything was covered with dust.

But her father had *not* been suddenly called away. He had simply stopped. She remembered how he had tried to sell the candy business. How no-one wanted it. André and Claude eventually ate what was left of the inventory.

Why had he never come down to put his affairs in order? Perhaps he could not bear to see the desolation, Nicole thought, staring at the broken, gaping drawer.

Once, she had been his helper, unpacking cartons, arranging the candy shelves, these very shelves that were now filled with junk. How important she had felt in the old truck, how indispensable, riding with her father, the Candyman, from store to store. It seemed so long since they had been friends. And yet, he had asked for her; the nurse had said so. He had wanted to see her.

She dusted off a few papers. An old bill for 25 cartons of potato chips. A receipt for a return shipment of conversation hearts. Was this all that was left of his life? She explored a drawer. There seemed to be no order, everything was muddled, confused. In the back of the middle drawer she found pencil stubs, an old pen, a dried up bottle of blue-black ink. Then, a rumpled carbon copy of a letter to the Department of Fisheries requesting a job. It was written in July 1947—she would have been two and a half then, she calculated—and in it her father listed all the things he had done. He had been an interpreter, a manager; he had helped start co-operatives among farmers, fishermen; he had a Bachelor's degree from Tufts University in Boston; before the Great Depression he had worked as an engineer.

All her life she had thought of him only as the Candyman, then as the old man who made her life and her mother's life miserable. She remembered the creditors who had hounded her mother because of his bills, threatening first to take the house and then to take the furniture, while her father sat in his chair with a newspaper, saying he had done his best and the creditors could all go to hell. Yet he had done so many interesting things. Things she hadn't known about. In her sociology class she had learned about the cooperative movement; why hadn't anyone told her he'd been a part of all that?

Stunned by the magnitude of her discovery, she dug into the other drawers, looking for more. She sifted through the filmy carbons, as thin and fragile as onion skins—bills, invoices, letters to attorneys and insurance companies. She was struck by the terrible struggle of it all, the crushing details of lost orders, minor accidents, robberies. She had been there, she had lived through it, yet it seemed different now, viewed through these pieces of paper—so many complications, so many impediments to success. Finally, she found what she had begun looking for without realizing: a personal letter addressed to her mother in her father's handwriting. Full of guilty curiosity, she took the letter from the envelope and read.

"Ma Petite Mignonne," it began. She had to read each sentence several times, as she was not used to reading handwritten French. He had gone to Halifax to attend some kind of meeting, she gathered, for he reported that it was going well. It was spring, for he talked about the flowering trees in the Public Gardens and how he wished she could see them. It made his heart ache, he said, to see those trees without her. After they were married and moved to Halifax, he would take her there for long walks. The letter was three pages long. Hope, joy and love leaped from her father's angular, gently sloping hand.

Nicole stared at the letter, trying to recall the early days when she was a child. But the pictures she remembered most clearly were the more recent ones: her father alone in his chair, the invisible wall that surrounded him, the disappointment, the anger, the failure. And yet, somewhere, behind all that, there had once been this. He had noticed things. He had felt things. He had had a life before them. And she had thrown him away, like a shabby old box, not knowing what was hidden inside. All those ugly things she had said to him, the times she had wished him dead!

The next day during visiting hours, Nicole held the limp packet of connected bones that was her father's hand.

"Dad, it's me, Nicole," she urged. "Please come back! I need to ask you something. I need to tell you something."

Between visiting hours she sat at the cluttered desk in the basement and wept.

For six days she sat at her father's bedside holding his hand, trying to call him back from wherever he was. Once his hand tightened on hers. *Dad, do you know it's me?* And for a moment she was sure he did.

When it was time to return to college she thought: it might have been only a spasm, the muscles involuntarily tensing.

In mid-November a call came to her dorm room in the middle of the night, and Nicole returned to Halifax. They rode in a long black car, she and her mother and André and Claude. Annette and Emile followed in another car, part of a long line of cars that followed them like a feast-day processional. It all seemed unreal, with those thin flurries of snow, as fine and dry as ashes, floating against the windows. Along the Bedford Highway, a group of workmen digging by the side of the road paused by their picks and shovels and took off their hats. Seeing them, their bare heads slightly bowed, their faces red and weatherbeaten, their woollen hats crushed against their chests—something inside her moved, flopped like a fish on the bottom of a boat. Beyond, the Bedford Basin shimmered pale and silent like the sky.

Later, they stood around a gaping hole while Father Casey spoke of resurrections, reunions. His red hair gleamed ferociously, obscenely, against the grey of the day, the drabness of their clothing, the dark pile of displaced earth. A birthmark on the side of his jaw, the shape and colour of a small clam shell, moved as his mouth moved, oddly, hypnotically.

Her mother stood very still, her face a mask. André stared at the hole; Claude's left foot twitched. Annette, pale and pregnant, leaned on Emile's arm, her big belly protruding from her open coat.

The others—who were they? She recognized Sam Dugas, his forlorn, rumpled face like that of a faithful dog, but the rest? Old business friends? Customers? It surprised her that her father knew so many people, that so many people cared about him. It didn't matter anymore. Nothing mattered except that hole, that deep, rectangular mouth into which he would go. It was neat and precise, the corners carefully squared as if it had been cut from the earth with a giant cookie cutter. She found herself wondering about the men who had dug it. Had they sat on the rim halfway through, drinking hot coffee, admiring their work?

Afterward, on their way back to the car, her mother took her arm. "Your father and I *did* love each other," she said emphatically, almost defiantly. "Things just happen." Her mother's nose was pink from rubbing.

But it didn't matter anymore. They had lowered him into that perfect hole and it was over.

All but the unknowing. The unknowing that gnawed at her for months, that seized her at unexpected moments, like sickness on a tossing boat. Had he felt her presence in the hospital-room? Had he heard her silently begging his forgiveness? Had he cared that she had come back?

In the five years since then, the mood of that day has settled on other days, as a cloud of smoke will drift anonymously from one town to the next, no longer associated with its origin. Nicole sits in her chair, staring at the grey sky, thinking only of her throbbing tiredness. Perhaps she will lie down after all. Surely she is tired enough to sleep soundly. Her limbs feel so heavy...

And lovely and inviting are the flannel sheets, the down comforter. Her face sinks into the pillow; everything smooths out, the release warm and liquid. Time passes.

Wait. Suddenly the mind snaps loose like a light flashing on in a dark room. *There's a noise in the hall.*

Don't be silly. It's only the wind, the cold, the house creaking.

There is someone here. Someone is coming down the hall.

You are imagining things.

Wake up. I need your eyes!

The body, heavy as earth, refuses to stir.

I know that shuffle, those slow, heavy steps. I know that rasping breath like the roar of the sea. Has he come to chastise me? Arms and legs, eyes, you must wake up!

He stops at the bedroom doorway. She feels him watch her sleeping body. Taut with fear, she waits for his judgment. Years pass. Her soul quivers, suspended. Finally, he moves on. Almost immediately, she jerks awake, blood pounding in her ears. Was it really him? She searches the empty hall on trembling legs for a sign, something physical. Surely it was a dream. It had to have been a dream. But what did it mean when the dead came like that? Suddenly, a clap of terror, sharp as lightning. *The baby. Something has happened to the baby!* She rushes wildly to the bedroom.

But she finds him sleeping peacefully, his fingers folded together like nesting birds. Only the drumming of her heart fills the room, so loud it will surely wake him.

She studies the little chest rising and falling, the eyes fluttering in dreams, and is astounded by the intensity of her fear. Astounding, too, is this surge of ferocious love she feels—for this little creature who troubles her nights, who occupies all her days, from whose life her own has become barely distinguishable. *This is what it means to have a child. What joins us is beyond words, beyond will or reason. This is what it means.* And in this moment, full of this knowing, she thinks of her father, now, after all those years of love and hate and grief, drawn to her doorway, just to watch her sleep.

yo
1994 Birthday...
to quote Sir William Osler:
"Nothing will sustain you more in
than the power to recognize in
your humdrum routine," the
true Poetry of life.
Since your routine is NEVER humdrum
Then you have "true poetry" in your life.
        Love,   [signature] 12/7/94